Confessions
of a Dandy

Confessions of a Dandy

Timothy G. Cates

Pentland Press, Inc.
England·USA·Scotland

PUBLISHED BY PENTLAND PRESS, INC.
5122 Bur Oak Circle, Raleigh, North Carolina 27612
United States of America
(919)782-0281

ISBN: 1-57197-124-6
Library of Congress Catalog Card Number 98-065644
Copyright 1998 Timothy Cates
Printed in the United States of America

To my Aunt Jo Nell, whose constructive criticism helped remove many mistakes from this book.

TABLE OF CONTENTS

ACKNOWLEDGMENTS

During the course of preparing *Confessions of a Dandy*, my editor, Drollene P. Brown, became my friend. Without her expertise and encouragement, this book would not exist. Although she was honest in telling me that her search for answers had not yielded the same conclusions I have reached, her belief that my work was valid buoyed my spirits in the bleakest of times. She has been more than a cheerleader, however. Her skill with the written word shaped my papers into a form that could be presented to the world, yet she retained my voice throughout. For all of her help, I am deeply grateful.

INTRODUCTION

Can one choose to be spiritual, or is each of us predestined to follow a certain path? The following papers were written as I searched for the answer to that question. I did not write out of desire, but out of compulsion. I had—and have—no choice.

After serving in the U.S. Army and attending college on the GI Bill, I taught high school biology in my home state, North Carolina. Diagnosed with schizophrenia at age thirty-eight, I eventually was given a medical retirement. I have been committed to institutions twelve times.

During my years of tribulation and survival, I have sought the truth by looking at my past, analyzing what others have told me, reading widely, and remaining sensitive to my own body and mind. Through all of these activities, I seek God's wisdom. I believe he is revealing his truth to me.

When I speak of Lefts and Rights in the following pages, I am not referring to politics. The division between Lefts and Rights that has been revealed to me is one of spirituality—or lack of it. The Rights have it; the Lefts do not. It is as simple as that. I have come to believe that you cannot choose what you will be, and it is not necessarily inherited. Worse, you cannot change it.

I am a Left. I am also a dandy. I do not know yet whether all dandies are Lefts, but one day I may figure it out, with God's help. I invite you to join my search for truth. Much of my writing may seem disjointed, skipping from one topic to another rather abruptly at times. That is in keeping with the subject matter. In order to explain some experiences, I must leap from one scene to another, then back again—as in a conversation with a friend.

Here is your chance to explore the mind of a Left, a schizophrenic, a dandy. Perhaps they are all the same. Enter if you dare.

PAPER ONE
What Is Truth?

PART ONE:

Scratching the Surface

There are age-old maxims that hint at truth:

"Language has not the power to speak what love indites: The soul lies buried in the ink that writes."

"The pen is mightier than the sword."

"God give me the courage to change the things I can change, to accept the things I cannot change, and the wisdom to know the difference."

"We should be found as liars. Truth is still the only safety."

–SOPHOCLES

"To Him that overcometh will I give to eat of the hidden manna, and will give him a white stone, and in the stone a new name written, which no man knoweth saving He that receiveth it."

–Revelations 2:7

My earliest memories began at my grandfather's house when I was about eighteen months old. My mother's hobby was photography, and she took many pictures of me when I was an infant and toddler. In pursuit of a photograph when I was about 18 months old, my mother made me stand on the running board of a dilapidated old car. I sensed that something was wrong, so I stepped down and moved away from the old wreck several times, but each time I was placed back on it. Finally, she got her picture. For another photograph she made me stick my thumbs in my ears and appear as a jackass.

Also about this time my aunt tried to give me a white stone. I would have none of it. While I am not sure of the significance of the white stone and my aversion to it, the symbolism of the old wreck and the little boy on the running board is quite apparent. I must be true to that little boy, and that is what I am trying to do as I write these papers.

When I was five years old my mother taught me two songs. The first: "Rock-a-bye-baby in the tree top, when the wind blows the cradle will rock. When the bough breaks the cradle will fall, and down will come baby cradle and all." The other: "One little, two little, three little Indians, four little, five little, six little Indians, seven little, eight little, nine little Indians, ten little Indian boys." In each successive verse an Indian boy is dropped. Therefore, there are no Indian boys at the end of the song. The loss or disappearance of the children in both these songs must have had some relevance to my mother's feelings about me.

How can a young boy make straight A's in the first grade and flunk the twelfth grade? Family events brought that change in me. When I was about seven years old, my parents separated. My mother raised me and my father "got religion." I was mad at my mother and said I was going to kill myself. She said that she would kill herself, too. She poured what I later realized was baking soda into a glass of water. She drank the solution and told me that she would be dead in a few minutes and now it was my turn. I didn't drink the mixture.

When I was still very young, my father told me that he would sacrifice me if God told him to. Where was this little boy's security? I certainly didn't find it with my parents, and there was no solace at school, either. In the elementary school grades the pupils would play softball almost every day during play period. The best players chose sides by alternately choosing the other players. I was the only boy never chosen. While the others played, I walked by myself around the school grounds in circles, day after day, month after month, year after year.

My mother told me that when she called me I must immediately stop what I was doing and run to her as quickly as possible. When she called me and I heard her, it was like electricity running through my body. She made a "coat of many colors" for

Confessions of a Dandy

me to wear. Time and time again my father reminded me that Joseph had a "coat of many colors." Joseph was sold into bondage by his brothers.

High school was not much better than the earlier grades. As would be expected, I had a king size identity crisis in high school. There was a room in which students danced after lunch. I never danced. I never had the opportunity to dance. At that point I realized that certain people can dance and other people cannot dance! Perhaps that was my first inkling that people were divided into Lefts and Rights.

When I was about eighteen years of age, I was invited by some older boys to go with them to a dance. I didn't know how to approach a girl so I became a "wallflower" and listened to the music. A boy I went with brought a girl over to meet me. He said to the girl, "I want you to meet somebody," and pointed at me. Then she, too, pointed at me, and they both laughed.

I did not understand the world and the world did not understand me. I had to invent my own world.

Most cultures have a ceremony or activity that serves as a rite of passage for boys. This rite serves to escort the boy into manhood. I never had any such help, so my transition (if it occurred at all) was very rough.

As I contemplate all that I had to learn on my own, I realize that I received much knowledge from an art book edited by Rockwell Kent, *World Famous Paintings* (New York Wise & Co., 1939). A picture by Raeburn, Plate 61, "Boy with a Rabbit," is accompanied by the comment, "Is this young manhood as we'd have it? We Americans must have our say—one page of *Huckleberry Finn* for all the Raeburn boys on earth."

When I was in the eighth grade my mother gave me my one page of *Huckleberry Finn* to read. In this passage was the scene in which Tom Sawyer and Becky Thatcher are trapped in a cave. Between them and the cave entrance is mean, old Injun Joe. Tom says he will protect Becky, and tells her that he loves her. When I read this as a boy, a funny feeling came over me. This must have been my rite of passage. Raeburn's "Boy with a Rabbit" must serve a similar purpose.

Plate 63 shows a picture by Lawrence, "Portrait of Master Lambton." Kent's comment: "Little Charles William Lambton— people of Byron's England loved to believe that boys were just like that."

The comments after plates 61 and 63 show a difference in cultural orientation. What is the great difference between the two paintings? Obviously there are differences, and I suspect that the primary one is of a spiritual nature. One subject is rich in spirit and the other is poor in spirit; guess which is which.

A painting by Perroneau, Plate 41, "Girl With A Cat," is interesting to me, partly because of the way others have viewed it. This picture of a girl with a cat has been ridiculed because the subject is not spiritually Right. Critics refer to her as a nincompoop.

Plate 74, "Hope," by Watts, depicts an older child—gender is not defined—on a large globe. The subject is bound and blindfolded. A copy of this very popular painting hung in my grandfather's office when I was young. It symbolizes young people and their fate if they are not spiritually correct.

In a painting by Pettie, "Two Strings To Her Bow" (Plate 84), two boys, one on each side of a girl, are called dandies. The subliminal sexual connotation in this picture is apparent upon study. The two dandies are Raeburn's boys. I relate to them, for I am a dandy, too. My grandfather, whom everyone called "Uncle Pill," referred to me as a dandy when I was young. When all is said and done, dandy means death.

In Plate 46, LeBurn's "Madame Vigee LeBurn and Her Daughter" is shown. From the commentary about this picture, we learn that the daughter married a certain M. Nigris. Nigris implies one of Raeburn's boys, or a dandy. I was a Nigris to two wives.

Here is what Coleridge wrote about the dandies, or the "poor in spirit"–"Apostrophize a Young Ass: innocent fool! Thou poor despised forlorn! I hail thee brother—spite of the world's scorn!" The "hail" in this passage translates "hell." The ass represents dandies!

Many little girls attend charm school. There, to make them ready for society, they are taught to induce thoughts and behavior in their peers. Here is Robert Burns' definition of society: "studied in arts of hell, in wickedness refined."

Some spiritual people throw what are known as "stumbling blocks" in the paths of those less fortunate than they. These blocks are not necessarily physical. When you begin to make a statement and someone interrupts you and you forget what you were going to say, this is a stumbling block. Some spiritual people can practically shut your brain down.

In this paper I will show the difference between spiritual and non-spiritual people, a disparity which has been cleverly hidden by the spirituals through the centuries.

6   *Confessions of a Dandy*

A definition of *lamb* is somebody who is easily taken advantage of. The word some*body* refers primarily to those people who are "poor in spirit." The word some*one* refers to those people who have the spirit. The same distinction applies to any*body* and any*one*. One term is discriminate, the other term is indiscriminate. The *lambs* are the poor in spirit and are very much taken advantage of by the spiritual people. The spiritual people can influence the lambs to do almost anything. They can even put ideas into their heads. An old English saying is this: "Stone walls and iron bars do not a prison make." If you are a dandy, the spiritual people have your mind in a trap that only God can open.

I have come to refer to the spiritual people as Rights and the nonspiritual people as Lefts. Most Rights are theist, that is, they believe in one or more gods. Most Lefts are confused, thanks to the Rights, and do not know what to believe. I will try to show this to be true, with information from writings in the Bible and by Western writers.

First, from the Bible:

"A wise man's heart is at his right hand, but a fool's heart is at his left."

–Ecclesiastes 10:2

"But when thou doest alms let not thou left hand know what thou right hand doeth."

–Matthew 6:3

[God told those who were at His left hand:] "Depart from me ye cursed into everlasting fire prepared for the devil and his angels."

–Matthew 25:41

One of the poets' and the Bible writers' favorite symbols is "O." The "O" means eternity, much as a ring means eternity. The "O" refers to man, not men. "Oh!" is used for men.

Another term used frequently by poets and the Bible writers is "Amen." "Amen" literally means without men. As I was contemplating this term, a very intelligent old man—both of his sons are doctors—called me on the phone and told me that his church quit using the term "Amen" three years earlier. How did he know exactly what I was thinking at that particular time?

A few more terms that exclude men are "brother," "sister," "mother," and "father." These terms represent mankind, not men. I suspect that there are other terms that are interchangeable, such as sun and son, sole and soul.

Men function with their brains and their senses. They just don't have mankind's "gifts."

It is not within the scope of this paper to discuss all of the philosophies or religions. Only one—Christianity—is addressed, although others are mentioned from time to time. The Christians believe in reincarnation, hence eternal life.

The following are lines from the Methodist Hymnal which were not written for men:

"Father love is reigning o'er us, brother love binds man to man."
"Christ the only true light; Sun of righteousness, arise."
"We lift our hearts to thee, O day-star from on high." (Notice the "O.")
"His glories shine with beams so bright no mortal eye can bear the sight."
"High in the heavens eternal God, thy goodness in full glory shines."
"Shed on us from above thine own bright ray."

Also, "Christ in me" and "living fire" appear many times in the hymnal. All of these lines were written for man, not men. Here's one that is for men: "they cannot reach the mystery." If I read this hymnal with no prior knowledge of Christianity, I would conclude that the people who use this book are sun worshippers.

Another line from the hymnal states, "That we fail not man nor thee." Notice "man" is used, not "men." Two other lines are, "A never ending soul to save and fit it for the sky," and, "From victory to victory till every foe is vanquished."

These lines sound suspiciously like Khrushev's speech to the United Nations many years ago: "We may not bury you all, but our children's children will bury your children's children." I once heard a preacher mention this in a sermon. I also heard a Satanist tell me this just before he planned to sacrifice me. I escaped by the grace of God.

How could Satanists and Christians say the same thing? Here is what Shelley has to say. He believed that man is essentially good and that truth would ultimately win. "The brotherhood of man is an attainable reality," he declared. Is something left out? How about men?

Let us look at some of Blake's writings. "Perfect unity cannot exist but from the universal brotherhood of Eden. The universal man to whom be glory evermore. Amen." The important part of this statement is the "Amen." "Glory" is one of the many states of immortality.

Blake also said, "I care not whether a man is good or evil, all I care is whether he is a wise man or a fool." The wise man can be good or evil. Blake declared, "We were placed here by the universal brotherhood and mercy with powers fitted to circumscribe this dark Satanic death." Men are not included in this brotherhood and mercy. The poet also proclaimed: "All that can be annihilated must be annihilated. This is a false body, an incrustation over my immortal spirit, a selfhood which must be put off and annihilated always." Nothing but reincarnation.

Another statement by Blake–"Looking on the rising sun: There God does live." Blake did not think very much of men; he wrote, "I have chosen the serpent for a counselor and the dog for a school master to my children."

In English literature, men are depicted as all kinds of animals, primarily dogs, jackasses, and swine.

Turning to Wordsworth, we read, "Who do thy work, and know it not: Oh! If through confidence misplaced. They fail thy saving arms, dread power! Around them cast." Also, he wrote: "My head has its coronal [crown]."

Shelley penned these words: "A portion of the eternal, which must glow through time and change unquenchably the same, whilst thy cold embers choke the sordid hearth of shame." "Hearth" in this passage really means "heart." You guess the rest! Again, Shelley writes, "Man, oh, not men! A chain of linked thought, of love and might be divided not. Man one harmonious soul of many a soul, whose nature is its own divine control."

Keats declared, "Glories infinite haunt us till they become a cheering light"—infinite reincarnations.

Here is more of the same from Tennyson: "To rust unfurnished, not to shine in use! As tho' to breathe were life. Life piled on life." And again: "Men may come and men may go but I go on forever."

Donne advised, "Virtue in woman see, and dare love that, and say so too, and forget the He and She." The soul is neuter! More Donne, from "Phoenix Riddle": "By us, we two being one, are it. So to one neutral thing both sexes fit, we die and rise the same, and prove mysterious by this love."

Whitman, in "Journeys Through the States," proclaimed, "We confer on equal terms with each of the states." Reincarnation again. Another from Whitman: "Here is the test of wisdom. Wisdom is not finally tested in schools, wisdom cannot be passed from one having it, to another not having it, wisdom is of the soul, is not susceptible of proof, is its own proof." Man versus men.

In Whitman's poem titled "Pioneers! O Pioneers!" each verse ends with the words of the title, "Pioneers! O Pioneers!" Here are two different types of pioneers. In some of Whitman's works, his use of "I," the personal pronoun, may refer to the poet as an individual or to Whitman himself, the unit of manhood, speaking for all mankind.

Robert Browning wrote, "Such feasting ended, then as sure an end to men. Then shall I pass approved a man, for aye removed from the developed brute; A god through in the germ." And Emily Bronte declared, "What loves me, no word of mine shall e'er betray." It just did!

This is just scratching the surface.

PART 2

Eyes Right

I was drafted into the U.S. Army by President Kennedy in December 1963. I took my basic training at Fort Jackson, South Carolina.

A part of basic training that stayed in my mind was having to go into a gas chamber filled with a deadly gas, chlorine. We were to "clear" our gas masks. Only a few of us were subjected to this. At the door to the chamber was a little man wearing a drill instructor's hat and dressed in civilian clothes. When I arrived inside, the little man was standing behind me to my left. He had no gas mask. I looked up, straight ahead, and I thought I saw gas. Or was it a spirit? A spirit looks like gas. Was this my first death?

"He that overcometh shall not be hurt of the second death."
—Revelations 2:11

Another strange thing happened to me while I was stationed at Fort Bliss, Texas. An artist drew my portrait in pencil, but I didn't want it because it showed me with a cigarette in my mouth. The artist took the picture to the owner of a bar, and they discussed it at length. How on earth could this picture have been so important?

Most of the time that I was in the U.S. Army I was stationed at Turner A.F.B. in Georgia. I was physically very large and very strong. One day I was entering the commissary and a small, young soldier bumped my shoulder. I gave him a little shove. He shoved back. I shoved him several times and he kept coming back. I finally went into the commissary. He would not give up. This man was a Right.

Tennyson said, "One equal temper of heroic hearts, made weak by time and fate, but strong in will to strive, to seek, to find, and not to yield." After the Vietnam War there were more than 1,500 soldiers unaccounted for. Why does our country forget about these soldiers? Maybe they are not Rights, not important enough to influence foreign policy. Quoting the Koran:". . . And hasten the destruction of the wrongdoers."

I attended college on the G.I. Bill. I was bigger and stronger and could jump higher than anyone trying out for the basketball team, yet I got cut. I know why, now. It was because I am a Left.

An athlete who sat beside me in an English literature class asked me to position my papers so that he could see the answers. I did so, but now I realize that I was the person who was being monitored.

Later, as a graduate student, I enrolled in a course called Field Botany. An old botanist was the teacher. He was more like a guru than a teacher. Over a period of time, we covered the state of North Carolina, camping out. There were two Lefts in the class; I was one of them. The students not only studied plants, they studied the human "bush."

When I graduated from college I immediately got a job teaching school in Guilford County. I did not do a very good job my first two years, but I became better each successive year.

In the fall of 1977, I received a call from a musician whom I had not seen in many years. He wanted to see me and invited me to come to his house. Little did I know that he and his friends were Satanists. In fact, his big, black Doberman was named Satan. When I realized that they were planning to sacrifice me, all the things that had happened to me began to fall into place.

When I arrived I saw eight straw dolls on a shelf. I asked what they represented and he replied, "You wouldn't understand. My girlfriend is making another one now." I immediately realized that it was mine that she was making. I escaped by the grace of God. That was only one of many attempts on my life. I cannot be killed unless God wills it.

After reading the Satanic Bible, I now know how Satanists choose their victims. They choose among people who are Lefts—

the ones who have low self-esteem and are obnoxious—the people who don't like themselves. Since these people do not like themselves, the Satanists consider it doing them a favor to kill them.

As you might expect, I was terrified after I escaped, and the terror did not wear off. I became paranoid. I told my "friends" about what had happened to me, and some of them laughed. Now I realize that if they believed the attempt on my life was bad; they thought it was worse that I escaped.

PART 3

The Bughouse

One day, when I was about six years old, I was sitting in the sandy soil at my grandfather's house. I looked up at the light, and I felt something in my chest. I felt that I was somebody; I was truly innocent.

A picture by Reynolds (*World Famous Paintings*, Plate 57), "The Age of Innocence," depicts a very young girl (a Left) pressing her hands to her breast and looking up toward the light. Commenting on this picture—and Reynolds' art in general—Blake wrote: "Reynolds' work is all time for the Satanists."

I was introduced to the spirit world when I was eighteen years old. I went to Southern Pines to see a female medium with my mother, a doctor, an intern, and some businessmen and their wives. Some people had to switch chairs to get the spirits "balanced." The spirit that used the medium's vocal cords was a Doctor Brookshire. He was a Scottish physician who spoke in a thick Scottish brogue. He had his physical death in about 1850.

At the end of the seance Dr. Brookshire allowed each of us a question. I, being young and stupid, asked, "Could you tell me how old I am?" He fired back, "Don't you know?" Then he said, "I'm not here to be tested but to impart truth."

A place where I wasted my life was the pool room, which is a metaphorical pool. It is where the sharks (good pool players) meet the fish (poor pool players). This is, of course, a Right-Left situation. I drank a lot of beer in the pool room and bought a lot of people beer. I thought I had a lot of friends in the pool room. In fact, I had no friends there; I had arch-enemies. One in particular, I'll call Surly.

Surly told me many times, "You don't know how you look until you have your picture took." Just before I had my "breakdown," I was in the pool room and I looked out the window. I saw a short, little, fat man with a huge flash camera. He took my picture. During my years of tribulation, I had my picture taken many times when I was not expecting it. I can understand Howard Hughes's aversion to cameras.

One of Surly's favorite sayings was "Let the whoop cord whoop." This is a little cryptic, but to me it represents my umbilical cord and my relationship with my mother. Another of Surly's favorite expressions was "Woo, woo, Chattanooga."

Surly knew the future. When I was young I had an electric train. I worshipped that train. A year or so before Surly's death, people in the pool room would ask me if I liked trains. I, of course, said yes. Then they would laugh.

After Surly's death, I married a girl from Saxapahaw. One day two of my "friends" were talking to me and one of them started to leave. Turning back, he said, "I must go to Saxapahaw to catch a train." There are no railroad tracks within twenty miles of Saxapahaw. A few days later I was crossing some railroad tracks and for some unknown reason I stopped . . . directly on the tracks. I looked up and there was a train bearing down on me, not more than fifty feet away. I escaped death by inches.

Then, a year or so later, I was not paying much attention to my driving and I suddenly drove over a railroad crossing much too fast and I broke both brake lines and lost my brakes. I made it safely.

Coincidence?

Another thing that Surly would say was, "When I get to hell, I hope that I am in charge of the water fountain, because I won't give that S.O.B. a single drop." He would crook his index finger as if holding a drop of water, but he was actually pointing at me.

Becoming paranoid made me a perfect candidate for witchcraft. The day of my "breakdown" at school the Satanists were driving me insane. One example of their work was the drawing of a dinosaur on the board with my name under it. We had just studied the extinction of dinosaurs. One of my students sat at his desk and was swatting at something and said, "This is as easy as swatting flies." Through my years of teaching, several little boys had approached, stomped the ground in front of me, and twisted their foot as if they were squashing a bug.

In the school where I taught there were about thirty students who were Satanists. Within a few days of the beginning of the onslaught, the witchcraft had driven me mad. I saw spirits come in the window. If all you have to work with is your five senses, you are dead. The Satanists are Rights, and so are the Christians. The Christians at the school gave the Satanists a little help, but they didn't need it. The faculty were almost all Rights.

"I looked for pity and found none."

–Psalms 69:20

On previous occasions I had noticed that some of the students at the school had scratched the eyes out of the pictures of people who were in magazines. I don't think I would be presumptuous if I labeled these students Satanists. People who have borrowed money from me through the years have almost never paid me back. That is the nature of things: Rights do not repay loans from Lefts. Blake said, "It is easier to forgive an enemy than to forgive a friend. The man who permits you to injure him deserves your vengeance: He also will receive it; go spectre! Obey my most secret desire." The Left permits his injury.

On the day the Satanists succeeded in driving me mad, I looked out the window and saw a spirit come in through the open window. I saw it go around the classroom, then it entered my head. I flipped out. I walked out in the school yard and I could hear grinding in my ears, such as the gnashing of teeth. I then went to the office and was promptly taken into custody by the sheriff's department. I was handcuffed and taken to the Guilford County Mental Health Department.

Then, strange things began to happen.

I was placed in the back of a van with a cage in front of me so that I could not escape. There was only one man other than me in the van, and that was the driver. Although I was in tribulation, I know what happened. We stopped at the highway patrol station and took on a most unusual passenger, a little man dressed in black, with a black cloth over his face. He got into the front seat with the driver, and we left for Umpstead. I was clutching a Bible. The little man in black would occasionally turn his head and look at me. I was petrified.

Why was the little man's face covered? Was he someone I might recognize? Was he the devil? When we arrived at Umpstead, the little man in black immediately jumped out of the van and ran away.

There were about a dozen orderlies waiting to handle me. They put me on a stretcher and rolled me down the hall. My eyes were closed tight. At the intersection of halls they spun me around and around about a dozen times. Then they took me to a little room with only one bed in it. They strapped me down. As soon as the orderlies left, a female nurse came in and fondled me. The technicians kept giving me shots to calm me down, but nothing worked. The next morning the psychiatrist looked at the chart showing all the drugs administered and couldn't believe his eyes.

There were some very unusual people down there, to say the least. One young African-American boy said to me, "You are a very important person." I replied, "No, I am not." He insisted, "You are very important to a whole lot of people." Then I thought, *The only thing about me that could be important is my soul!*

I went to the canteen one day and a very old lady sat down with me at a table. She started mumbling, and I thought she was crazy as a loon. She suddenly announced the exact amount of money that I had in my checking account. I did not know the amount myself, but I recognized it when she said it.

A few weeks before my breakdown I had been dating a girl. One evening when I was at her house she received a phone call. When she hung up she told me to leave and not come back. She knew that I was a marked man.

In my eleventh trip to a bughouse, I was taken to Chapel Hill: South Wing. This place was so secure that even doctors were not allowed in. Here is where ten days of tribulation took place. I was placed in a private room. I prayed without ceasing for ten days and ten nights. I prayed to God. I begged God to give me the power, and I would destroy the devil.

While I prayed I felt lifted out, but I looked up and saw three figures in white coats standing over me. One of them lifted my left eyelid and put something behind my eye. I felt no pain. Then hell came through my open door. I developed a headache. It was a permanent type of pain which lasted only a few moments. When hell was almost on me I cried out to God to save me. Hell and my headache disappeared.

Then a murky, green spirit entered my room. It looked like a hurricane as seen from space. It settled down on my face and tried to enter my brain. I fought it as hard as my brain could fight. I do not know whether this spirit entered my mind.

Confessions of a Dandy

On the tenth day of my tribulation at Chapel Hill, after no sleep at all, I finally told God, "Thank you for Jesus." Then a small, quivering red cross appeared in my mind. It was slowly rising above the silhouette of a hill. When the cross disappeared I fell into a deep sleep.

Another thing of interest happened to me at Chapel Hill. A psychiatrist approached me and talked to me in riddles. "When the big fish is in shallow water, the small fish play," he said, then asked, "What do you think of that?" He said, "The gold key unlocks the iron door," then asked again, "What do you think of that?"

One day a cook came out of the kitchen, and I looked at her from a distance of about fifteen feet. She was an African-American, but she appeared exactly like my mother.

On the way back from Chapel Hill we passed a large herd of cows, a hundred or so. They were all looking at me, and I was looking at them. Suddenly they all ran away from me. Stampede!

My grandfather was a surveyor, and when I was young we had occasions to be in cow pastures. If livestock were in the pastures they would always come after me. I sometimes had to climb a tree. Why would the cows always come after me? There were other people in the pasture that they ignored.

Another strange thing happened at Chapel Hill. I was sitting on the floor looking at my door and noticed a pattern on it. It was an exact replica of a scar on my shoulder that I had received in a fight. It was correct even to the looks of the lacquer, which appeared as blood.

While I was in Alamance Bughouse I had looked at a wall and it looked back. There were about twenty eyes staring at me. This is important because I know that particular vision originated in my mind.

When I was between tribulations I was invited to be an usher at a U.N.C. football game. During the game, I looked at the stands on the opposite side of the field. I saw almost everyone looking at me. Their eyes were very large, with a familiar, murky tint. The force knocked me backward. That was the reason I had been invited.

A year or so ago I was drinking coffee at a Waffle House. I looked up and there was a man, a woman, and a child staring at me. I have seen that look before. These eyes were like the eyes at the U.N.C. football game. I kept reading my paper and the man walked by me. Suddenly, as he passed, a molten, golden glow came over me and my booth.

On numerous occasions I have seen the evil eye on family and friends. Also, winking is frowned upon in the Bible.

Here is something that I find amusing: When I was in tribulation a boy told me that if a person found a penny and if it were on tails it would bring bad luck. Of course, over the following few years I found dozens of pennies on tails.

Another time when I was in tribulation I drove to Gettysburg. I don't know why. On the way back the car ran out of gas. I could not lie down to rest, for the car had bucket seats with a handbrake in between. After sitting there an hour or two I could see something in the distance. It looked like three figures. Each one was dressed in a robe and hood and had a shepherd's staff in his right hand. The beings came up to the car and just stood there. I stared at the tops of their staffs. The tops (like pinwheels) moved when I looked at them. Then the figures moved away to my right. I made it back home okay.

Between tribulations I ate breakfast at a cafe frequented by many people that I knew. Once I was in tribulation and was standing at the cash register. An old "friend" of mine drew a diagram of a grave and an arrow and said, "The only way out is six feet under and straight up." Then a guy I knew whose name was Daniel Webster told me that he had sold his soul to the devil. About this time I was taking a course at U.N.C.G. in which I studied subliminal influences. I was looking at an advertisement in a magazine. Suddenly something came over me and I realized the subliminal message. From then on I was an expert on subliminal messages.

My uncle would drink occasionally. He was drunk at my grandfather's house when he told my mother, "I hope your brain rots in hell." My mother and uncle were in another room, but I could see them. My uncle was pointing over his shoulder at me when he made that statement.

My father is a Gideon. He invited me to a Gideon meeting one morning. All the Gideons knelt, and I joined them. We took turns praying aloud. When it came my turn to pray I was in the spirit. I prayed for Jesus to come quickly. A great roar arose from the Gideons. It can only be described as a roar from hell. After praying, I stood up and observed one of the Gideons drawing something on a piece of paper. He was drawing perfect geometrical figures freehand—a human impossibility.

When I was in the Alamance Bughouse an old man dressed in black came in there. He was a very big and imposing man. He stared at me for, maybe, thirty minutes. When he left, I walked by the chair in which he had been sitting. I smelled a very strong, burnt cinder odor. I had smelled that odor one time before in my grandfather's office when I was a young boy.

After leaving Alamance I entered the day program at mental health. We would go on picnics every few days. I was sitting on a bench beside an old man when a hornet landed beside us. The old man said, "If you are afraid of that hornet, he will sting you." Is this true? More recently I walked out of the grocery store and through a large swarm of bees without being stung. I was not afraid.

While being driven home from day program, I was sitting behind the driver of the van. He was a rather large man. The van passed through some small branches. The sun was in our faces. Suddenly the driver reached for the sun with his right hand and held a sphere of very white light in the palm of his hand, appearing to "serve" it to me. He said, "This is what you get."

Once when I was in tribulation I was placed in a rescue unit. I closed my eyes tightly and saw the primary colors flash in my conscious mind. One of the attendants said, "We'll be back to get you in a couple of years."

Another time when I was in tribulation at my house, three times a bright white light flashed through my mind. It was like a flash bulb. Could this have strip-searched my mind for knowledge?

One day I was in tribulation and I went into the pool room. I could see what appeared to be Japanese lanterns (lights) over the heads of the people in there. These people were enlightened by the spirit. Some of them were not Christians.

Several years ago I had a heart attack, and I was flown to Duke Hospital. When I was in the operating room I could hear the doctors discussing my case. One of the doctors said, "I don't want it." Another one said, sighing, "I guess I'll take it." I had successful angioplasty.

Once when I went to the dentist, I was seated in the chair to be given Novocain. However, it wasn't Novocain that was given to me. The procedure was a root extraction, very painful. I could see hell closing in on me from both sides. A tiny boy dressed in white appeared in front of me, and hell disappeared. I kept my consciousness. I remain true to that little boy.

PART 4

Beating the Grim Reaper

"The awful shadow of some unseen power; floats through unseen among us," said Shelley. Whitman described certain men and women as "smartly attired, countenance smiling, form upright, death under the breastbone, hell under the skullbone."

Twenty-five years ago my wife lived at Virginia Beach. I would go to a bar in Virginia Beach while she was at work. I met a man there who said he was a teacher. I had no reason to doubt him. He talked at length about sublimation, the process in which matter changes directly from a solid state to a gaseous state, skipping the liquid state.

He asked me to go to his house to see his garden. I did. As I was looking out his back door I could see a patch of disturbed ground. When I turned around, the man had a hammer raised as if to strike me. I asked him, "What are you doing with that hammer?" He replied, "I was only moving it." This event happened before any tribulations that I experienced, but God revealed it to me long after they occurred.

As I was returning home from Gettysburg, I was in tribulation. I picked up a hitchhiker, and for some reason I kept one eye on him and the other on the road. He was with me about one hour. I suddenly pulled off the road and let him out; he seemed glad to get out. The next morning I discovered a dagger on my floorboard.

Between tribulations I dated a very pretty girl. This girl had "religion." At her house one day, she anointed my head with oil. She told me to get down on all fours. I did. Then she told me to bark like a dog. I did. Then she sat in a chair. Next she propped her feet upon my back. Then she said, "When are you going to stop letting the devil kick you around"? It seems to me that she did a good job of kicking me around herself. She would also sing in the "unknown tongue."

My father and I went to this pretty girl's church. We sat on the back row. A group of teenagers sat in front of us. Occasionally they would look at me. When they looked at me I felt fear in my heart, and they knew it. They smiled.

In 2 Timothy 4:3 is the admonition, "Beware of teachers having itching ears." When I was in this church my ears itched. A member of the church quoted that verse to me.

My cousin Arnold owns a store. On two occasions he took me to a Mexican bar. The first night he parked in front of the bar. There were about twenty Mexicans and their girlfriends in the bar. I waited in the truck. Arnold tried to get me to come inside, but I refused. The Mexicans came out of the bar with their heads down, a solemn procession. They all left. The same thing happened again about a week later.

After all this happened, God revealed to me in a vision what was going on. Arnold was trying to kill me. These two occasions were not the only times he tried it.

Some unusual things have happened at Arnold's store. Several years ago, I was there using the commode. When I stood up and flushed the commode it immediately was full of water. There were several people sitting around, one of them a magician. He said: "Don't you feel that noose tightening around your neck?" Then the devil came in. He conversed with Arnold for a few minutes and left.

About a year later I was in Arnold's store, and this is what happened. I was talking with three men, all of them my seniors, and again the devil showed up. As I arose and walked to the counter, the three men behind me began to curse. When I turned around to face them, they abruptly stopped. Then I left. The devil looks like an average person except for one thing: he can change himself into fire.

I will now simply touch on something that I will discuss at length later. Mas runs the store for Arnold. One day when I was seated in a chair about ten feet away from Mas and the counter, I

Confessions of a Dandy

noticed that occasionally a person would stop and communicate with Mas. I was to observe this many times in the ensuing years. What was so strange about this interaction? They communicated without the aid of the five senses!

One time I set a trap for Arnold. I told him that I didn't believe in "gifts." When he heard this he jerked violently.

A year ago I went with two of my "friends" to a bird strut. I lost money at this bird strut, but I also nearly lost my life. One "friend" insisted on staying later and later, but finally we left. Something was not quite right, or I would have been killed. God revealed this to me.

And now for my good "friend" Lunnie. The devil made him try to kill me on several occasions. He could not bring himself to do it, although he did slip me some angel dust once. Angel dust induces tribulation. Since Lunnie could not bring himself to kill me, the devil made him take his own life.

How can things be so bad in this life as to take a chance on something being worse in the next life (hell)? Do people who take their own life go to hell? Most Christians would answer "Yes" to this question. If man has an immortal soul, where does it go after death of the body? Christians know, although they won't admit it. Sanctified means their soul is predestined to another physical body—reincarnation.

Why is alcohol called spirits? I think that the effects of alcohol are such that they numb that part of the brain that makes us human, namely the cerebral cortex. This is where the spirits come in to play, for spirits are not human. Alcohol (spirits) can make a sane man do bizarre things, things that he would never do sober. An alcoholic can only stop drinking if God wills it.

Now let me mention the Boy Scouts. For two years, as a boy, I went to every meeting as a member of the Boy Scouts. The scoutmaster ignored me the whole two years. I never went past Tenderfoot. There was another boy in my troop who made Eagle and he got all the attention. Once, in school, I was in the front of the line and this same boy came up to me and pushed me out of line. I pushed back and the teacher sent me to the back of the line.

I was leaving Alamance Mental Health one summer day and about the time that I arrived at my car, a little African-American girl and her parents were walking by. The little girl was reaching toward my car and saying, "That's my car, that's my car." Her parents said, "That's right, but come on." They were an obvious trio of Rights. The Rights think they own everything. Some of this originates from the several covenants in the Bible, especially the Abrahamic. Some

Rights will purposely destroy the property of Lefts and pretend it was an accident. I could make a list here, but I won't. Suffice it to say it is fact.

Since I became grown, I have been in several altercations and won most of them. I have also had to "eat crow" several times. These times, I was put in a situation where I was damned if I did and damned if I didn't. Twice, when I was playing with a band at fraternity parties, "brothers" stood in front of me and called me every name in the book. They ignored the other men in the band.

While I was in tribulation, I went to the death bar. There I met Crip, whom I had known for many years. As I sat beside him, he told me that I had to go out. I knew too much, he insisted. I told him that I was different from other people, and he replied, "Yes, I know." He wanted me to play chess with him, but I told him that it would be checkmate in the game of life. He died a few weeks later.

After speaking to Crip, I hurried out the door, then paused for a moment. I saw a man and a woman standing in the shadow of the street light. I recognized the woman from the bughouse. She came toward me, fumbling in her pocketbook. I pointed my finger at her and she fell backward into the man. I quickly left.

I did not believe in ghosts until I saw several of them. The spectres that I saw were of people that I knew well. They were usually life size. Only Rights have spectres. Let us examine spectres by taking a look at the Salem witch trials. Exodus 22:18, "Thou shall not suffer a witch to live," was taken literally by the Puritans in seventeenth and early eighteenth century New England. Thirty-one women were either burned at the stake or hanged during this period.

Were witches actually there during that period? Yes! Were any executed? No! A woman proficient in the black arts can easily conceal her power. In one case, a woman was charged with witchcraft, and when she came into court two young girls threw themselves on the floor, shouted, and writhed around. The poor woman was found guilty and executed. The real witch sat in the congregation and laughed up her sleeve.

Another poor woman was hanged on the evidence of a spectre alone. The Rights were only too glad to hang a Left. Even two dogs were executed for witchcraft.

Here is an interesting story from Argentina. A priest in the Pampas tried to get the Indians who lived in the jungle to come to church. The gauchos laughed and refused to go to church with Indians. They considered the Indians dogs. The gauchos came up with a solution. They invited the Indians to a banquet. After the banquet, the gauchos shot the Indians and killed them all, twenty-three in number.

Plate 16 in *World Famous Art* shows "The Adoration of the Kings," a depiction of the Madonna and child, along with the kings. It also shows two dogs in the forefront. It does not take a rocket scientist to realize that the dogs represent the Lefts. The Lefts are slaves to the Christians and other Rights.

I have suspected for a long time that Rights can read the minds of Lefts. To test the hypothesis, I set up an experiment. I would occasionally go to this old hermit's house to drink beer. We were sitting in the front seat of my car and I turned my head away from the hermit and thought, *I believe I'll kill the hermit.* Immediately, he jumped out of the car.

Here is an example of the way Satanic doings are viewed by the press. Suppose a cow is found dead in a field. The blood is drained out of the cow, and maybe some organs are missing. Perhaps a podium is found at the site, in addition to other evidence that a ceremony had taken place. Newspaper editors and law enforcement agents explain it all away. Why? Because the authorities are Rights, the Satanists are Rights, the victims are Lefts. Need I say more?

There is a store in Alamance County that specializes in witchcraft paraphernalia. This store has an unbelievable stock. It has everything that a witch could possibly need to cast any spell. They do a brisk business.

The art book's Plate 96 shows "The Race Track." This golden glow picture of a ghostlike figure mounted on a horse, sickle in hand, signifies the cycle of death. It also represents life . . . for some.

PART 5

Contemporary Observations

"And you shall be betrayed both by parents, brethren, and kinfolk and friends."

–Luke 21:16

The 1960s movie "The Manchurian Candidate" was about mind control. A certain visual stimulus triggered a man to obey the next order that he heard. In this film the man was told to kill certain people, and he did. How much truth was in this movie?

I have the understanding that a person could not be made to do anything against his moral understanding (conscience). Here is what I have experienced regarding this topic. While camping out with other students and the old botanist (my graduate school "guru," mentioned earlier), the class parked the cars and walked down the path to the big rock at Big Rock. It seemed a short walk, maybe a hundred feet. Several years later I went back to Big Rock with my father. I had thought the rock was only a stone's throw from where we parked, but it was not where I thought it was. Although I had a perfect mental image of the rock, my father and I followed the trail on and on for at least a mile before we came to it.

One day when I was driving to Roche Laboratory, my car and I were instantly transported to another part of town. It is my opinion that many Lefts can be—and are—controlled in similar fashion.

Were these examples of attention deficit syndrome? Consider this: I can play, from memory, on the piano very difficult pieces of music—music that has thousands of notes—in just the correct sequence. Do I have a good memory?

Emotions can best be described as feelings. Facial expression and body position are used in much of the animal kingdom to convey visual messages. Humans are no exception.

Years ago, when I attended church, some of us would go outside and smoke. One of the deacons, who was also a smoker, would watch me out of the corner of his eye when I lit up. He was trying to put me on a guilt trip. This was not the only situation where this occurred.

The twelve-year-old daughter of a girl I dated did this to me. She told me that I was going to laugh. I tried not to, but I did. I had much better reason to cry. How could she control my emotions?

I am reminded again of the works of Mark Twain. The way Tom Sawyer got others to whitewash the fence for him is another important story. This episode, along with the previously mentioned cave scene, is partly why Mark Twain's works are so controversial among educators. Such tactics described by Twain is where the term "huckster" comes from.

Many years ago, I worked one summer on the highway. When the foreman would approach me he would always say: "Cul-de-sac, cul-de-sac," which means dead end. Another man who worked on the road said, "I am not going to work with that nigger." He cursed and cursed "that nigger." There was one elderly African-American on the job. I was given a job to do with him, but I refused, because of what the other man had said. Now I know that I was the nigger. I had been "huckstered."

P.T. Barnum said, "A sucker is born every minute." W.C. Fields said, "Never give a sucker an even break."

I took up golf about twenty years ago. I quit about ten years later. There were occasions when there was gambling. Here is a pattern that I noticed: when I would drive the ball off the tee, I never could connect properly with it. Each time I teed off, I noticed a particular player flinch as I struck the ball. Somehow, he influenced my swing. This happened literally hundreds of times. I am very well coordinated, but I could not get the ball off the tee.

Confessions of a Dandy

Another time while I was in tribulation I was at U.N.C.G. I had to sign a document and I tried hard to sign my name, but I couldn't. Instead I made the sign of infinity.

Now for a poker game. I have played poker for many years. Although I have a high I.Q., I have been a consistent loser. I have come to the conclusion that the devil has always been in the game. Other players have known what cards I had in my hand. Either they could see what my eyes saw, or they could see my thoughts. There is no other possible explanation. Science!

Now for money. Emily Bronte wrote, "No graven image may be worshipped except the currency." What is it about the currency that should be worshipped? Maybe it's the words! Let's look at the words on a dollar bill:

> In God We Trust
> Annuit Coeptis
> Novus Ordo Seclorum

> On the penny are the words E Pluribus Unum.

Here are the meanings of these words: annuit coeptis, beginning money; novus ordo seclorum, new government to hide. E Pluribus unum, one among many (to a man). One among many means one spirit, God, among many people (Rights). This explains almost all of the writings of English literature. The spirits of Rights are reincarnated at death into a new physical body.

One among many also explains much of what happens in everyday life. Farrikhan, leader of the Nation of Islam, claims that he has a spaceship orbiting the earth and some people are beamed up and down from it. This is true. The one among many makes all Rights astronauts.

My ex-nephew was a terrible student in school, and his mother said that he wanted to become an astronaut. She asked me several times, "Don't you have to have some college to become an astronaut?" I marveled at that question, but simply answered, "Yes." The truth is, he was already an astronaut. Right.

Rush Limbaugh makes fun of Farrikhan's statement about the spaceship, but he knows it is true. He is fooling the Lefts on this one.

One recent summer, my father, stepmother, and I spent the day at Pilot Mountain. When I returned, my good "friend" Lunnie said that he had been up there also. He insisted that he had been there. This was an attempt to confuse me, but it did not. I understood exactly what was truth.

Neil Armstrong said, "One small step for man, one giant leap for mankind." There was a countless number of spirits with him when he took that step. The poor Lefts were left out completely.

I could give numerous accounts of Rights reading the minds of Lefts, mine included. Rights can also plant thoughts in the minds of Lefts. I have very good evidence that the thoughts of Lefts can travel through phone lines. However, this could be that awful shadow of some unseen power that flows among us. I have seen this awful power.

Rights can monitor the thoughts of Lefts from miles away. In Ecclesiastes 10:20 we read, "Curse not the king or the rich in thy bed chamber for a bird shall carry your thought, and that which has wings shall tell the matter." Thoughts are electrical impulses which set up an electrical field around the body. The Rights have the ability to monitor this field. They can see the image formed by the minds of the Lefts.

The communications between Rights and Rights monitoring the Lefts involve several body parts: the larynx, tonsils, adenoids, brain, heart, and ears. I do not completely understand the functions of these structures, but I will.

I believe our government has a secret base in New Mexico where it studies the parameters of the spiritual world and electronics. The government claims it has no such base, but it does!

Let's look at Gypsies. They are dark skinned Caucasians that migrated from India to Europe in the fourteenth century. They are a very spiritual group of people. Here is what Matthew Arnold, a Victorian poet, said about Gypsies in his poem "The Scholar-Gipsy": "His mates had arts to rule as they desired. The workings of men's brains. And they can bind them to what thoughts they will."

Now let's look at the continuity of spirits. What happened to Hitler's spirit? When I was in tribulation, a boy told me that it was in Florida. When Hitler killed himself, his spirit must have gone somewhere. But where? And where are the spirits of the Great Masters? It is my contention that they are alive and well in the psyche of modern artists.

The Satanists seem to have the ability to avoid hell. How?

The Protestants, especially the Baptists, criticize Catholics, Mormons, Moslems, and other religions, but they never say a word against the Satanists. Let's look at this: the Baptists have a pulpit. The function of it is to allow the preacher to pull the people into the pit. Wisdom cannot be transferred from a person having it (Right) to a person not having it (Left).

Now let's look at the altar. The altar is where things are sacrificed to God. What is being sacrificed? I'll tell you; it is the poor Lefts. An altar call is a farce. The Satanists and most Christians are covertly working together. Both groups are Rights. Their goal is "no Lefts." Amen.

I have visited my sister-in-law and her husband many times. Often she would say something like, "There is a patrolman coming down the road." She could not see him. She could not hear him. She could not taste him. She could not smell him. She could not feel him. The only possible explanation for her knowing is extrasensory perception.

Her husband has said to me a number of times, "I can con if I want to." He is a Right.

Amil, a friend of my mother, told me just before he died, "Soon they will have places to put people like you."

Sometimes I drink coffee with Rights. I can bring up a subject that they know little about and they will excuse themselves and go to the rest room for a couple of minutes and come back to the booth with much knowledge on the subject being discussed. Sometimes the rest room trips are so frequent that it borders on comedy.

"One among many." I will give you a few more examples of this in action. A "friend" told me that he could press four hundred pounds. I knew that this "friend" could never press four hundred pounds, but a mutual "friend" could press four hundred pounds. They shared the spirit.

Another "friend" made the statement, "I can do anything as well as any*one* else can."

I have told jokes and noticed that Rights begin laughing before the punch line is complete.

Moreover, the Lefts are never given reinforcement, no matter how well they perform a task. They may occasionally receive a little lip service, but that is all. Take my piano playing, for example. No *one* actually appreciates my music. I am like a dog jumping through a hoop. If I intensely studied a piece of music, I would be like a dog jumping through two hoops. Because I am a Left, the Rights believe that I am fundamentally inferior. They do not have enough sense to realize that my piano playing is the real thing.

Several years ago a "friend" and I got drunk. He told me, "No *one* likes you. You are a joke." I didn't pay much attention to this at the time, but I have since come to realize that it is the truth.

Here is another example of mind reading. I was in a cafe recently and said to the waitress and cook, "I had to take that damn cat." I paused a moment and thought, *Excuse me, Lord (for cursing)*. When I thought that thought, the waitress and cook looked at me and laughed. They had read my mind. There are numerous examples I could give in which Rights have somehow received the pictures that I formed in my mind.

How about voodoo? Voodoo is nothing more than the African brand of witchcraft. It was brought to the Caribbean and the U.S. by slaves. Voodoo practitioners communicate with animals and cast spells on humans. Some of these people are called Zombies. Some of these Zombies are thought to have come back from the dead. There are certain stimuli that turn off some Lefts and other stimuli that turn them on again. I have been a Zombie. My own thought is that attention deficit syndrome is somehow involved.

How about the balancing of baskets by African women on their heads? How about the spinning of a basketball on some people's fingers? How about Slalom Skiing? How about jumping rope? There are many physical activities that Rights can do but Lefts can't. Somehow the Rights have better balance and coordination.

Let me mention the K.K.K. They sometimes attend meetings with their faces covered. The purpose of this is not to conceal the faces of the white members, but to conceal the faces of the black members. All K.K.K. members are Rights. Their victims are Lefts. Skin color has nothing to do with their activities.

One example of a stimulus response is this: I was in a spiritual battle with some Rights. I thought, *I've got the trump card*. Hooked to that thought was the question, *Why don't you play it?* They planted both of these thoughts. The Rights were in a no lose situation. If the thoughts took, good. If they didn't take, nothing was lost. Fishers of men?

No Left can read music very well, although a few can memorize it. Some Rights are excellent readers of music. The reason for this is that they have a much greater sense of body position than Lefts.

Let's look at politics and our form of government. By and large the lawyers control the precincts and, therefore, who is to run for office. The Lefts are influenced by the Rights about how to vote. The precinct workers and the controversial poll watchers are the culprits. A Left may think he originates his own thoughts, but that is not true.

How about the Satanists? Harley Davidson is the name of a very famous motorcycle. Through the years I have seen many shirts worn by the patrons of bars bearing the Harley Davidson logo. On the back of the shirts are the words "Harley Davidson Motor*cycle*" and a pair of wings. Now David-son means the son of David. Jesus was the son of David. The wings mean angels, the cycle means life cycle. The whole thing means immortality. The Satanists and the Christians are two sides of the same coin.

I might mention that there are different kinds of spirits, not just a good kind and a bad kind. The Bible mentions several spirits. How about animal spirits? I have often marveled at how flocks of birds and schools of fish turn in unison. This kind of behavior must depend on an electrical field (spirit), albeit a weak one. Twice I have observed expert fishermen find fish. They knew the fish were there. Spirits?

I have observed Rights come forth many times with information that could not be attributed to the five senses. Here is the reason that this can happen: E Pluribus Unum!

Here is an example of hucksterism with yet another twist. I was talking to a "friend" about a woman. He said, "She smells every time you get around her." That meant that she smelled me.

The use of the English language is full of such hokum. There is a shooting range a short distance from my house. People used to shoot all the time. Often it sounded like a war going on. About two months ago the shooting abruptly stopped. I don't know what stopped it, but about that time I thought to myself, *I am not afraid of those guns. God can force them to shoot themselves if he wants to.*

At this point I would like to mention an old man, the only person who ever gave me a quarter. He told me that he knew I had it rough. No one else even acknowledged the fifteen years of hell I had gone through. That's why I'm not afraid of hell; I've been through it.

Now a little science lesson: the three dimensions of space are height, width, and depth. What is the fourth dimension? People will tell you that it is time, but the real fourth dimension is spirit. Since the spirit is ageless, it could include time.

Once I touched a man's arm and saw his spirit jump out of him (coming from his head).

When I was at the beach with a "friend" of mine, I left the waitress a five dollar tip. He kept telling people that he was the one who left the tip. Who left it? About the same time I picked up a beautiful girl and took her to our room. No money was mentioned, but as she was leaving, I gave her twenty dollars. My "friend" said, "You paid for it."

Can human spirits enter other animals? The Hindus think so. I am not sure about this.

Something does strike me as odd. It is the huge hog farm beside Umpstead Hospital—a very peculiar place for a hog farm.

Cowards die a thousand deaths; the brave die but once. Being a Left and many times having fear in my heart, I might suppose that all Lefts are cowards. However, this is not true.

A "friend" told me that the U.S. soldier is the best soldier in the world, for U.S. soldiers have a much better chain of command and much better lateral communication. E Pluribus unum. There is a theory that everything in the universe is connected to everything else in the universe. I put this question to you: can a butterfly in Brazil cause a tornado in Kansas? I say it is possible, but the probability of this occurring approaches zero. What gives this idea plausibility is the dark unseen power that is everywhere. Almost.

Reincarnation and "one among many" are paramount to Rights. Their religions and philosophies are based on these two tenants.

Subliminal (covert) stimuli influence much behavior, as do overt stimuli. The different combinations of overt and covert stimuli can explain almost all of human behavior. The Rights' mastery of the five senses puts them in the "catbird seat" when dealing with the Lefts.

When I was about fourteen, my mother dated a very nice man. I wanted to match him with pennies. I put my coin on the table and he did, too. He had an incredible tactile sense. He asked me to show my coin first. Then he asked me to "call it." I missed him seven times in a row! The odds of this happening by chance are 128 to 1. The fact is that he knew what he had, and not only that, he influenced my call. That is why I missed the call seven times in a row. Was he a Levite?

A few quotes from English literature:

CLARE–"The heart and hope of man are infinite, heaven is his home, and, exiled here on earth complexion most betrays the incompleteness." Complexion means mode of thought.

ROSSETTI–"And sleep and wake and never break the chain."

BROWNING–"Sleep, dream a little, and get done with it, the sooner the better to begin afresh." Browning describing Lefts: "Lofty designs must close in like effects: Loftier lying, leave him—still loftier than the world suspects, living and dying."

DONNE–"Dull sublunary lover's love (whose soul is sense) cannot admit absence, because it doth remove those things which elemented it."

WHITMAN–"I too had received identity by my body. Keep your places, objects than which none else is more lasting."

Confessions of a Dandy

Rights literally resent the Lefts' breathing air. They also resent the space that the Lefts take up. When I am in front of a line, Rights try to make me as uncomfortable as possible.

Plate 62 of *World Famous Paintings* shows "Interior of a Stable," a picture of three horses in a stable being attended by two peasant men. The commentary says: "Morland's fondness for a subject such as this had perhaps the same motivation that prompts us—how ridiculously—to isolate seven days a year for 'be kind to animals week' when well we know that this idea of concentrating a virtue temporarily betrays the truth that we are not gentle in our treatment of living things as a general rule."

PART 6

The Left Writes

"What limit can be put to this power, acting during long ages and rigidly scrutinizing the whole constitution, structure, and habits of each creature, favoring the good and rejecting the bad? I can see no limit to this power, in slowly and beautifully adapting each form to the most complex relations of life."

—DARWIN

When taking a class at U.N.C.G., I was in a depressed mood. I told the professor I thought the human race would eventually become extinct. He replied, "No it won't, because man thrives in a subclimatic environment." I take issue with this statement. A study by Malthus titled "Essay on Population," a paper on human population growth that was published in the nineteenth century, predicted that at the rate of population growth at that time, there would be, by the year 2600, one square foot of land for each individual on this planet. According to Malthus, there are two ways to prevent this from happening: (1) controlled birth or (2) uncontrolled death. These are natural laws which will enforce themselves.

There are many theories on human evolution; attempts to explain man's superiority in nature. They are based on such things as the discovery of controlled fire, agriculture, the invention of the wheel, and even the anatomy and physiology of man. However, there is more going on in the evolution of man than meets the eye.

Let's look at agriculture. How did it start? Some teachers will tell you that the "hunters and gatherers" initiated agriculture by accident. One of the gatherers noticed a sprout growing where some seeds had been dropped. Once the connection between the seed and the plant was recognized, agriculture was born. When the ancient farmer could not only feed himself and his family, but two or three more people, the extra people could turn their energies to other endeavors. Division of labor leads to greater efficiency and specialization.

Where on this earth did modern man get his human soul? A recent article in *National Geographic* shows several possibilities: Europe, Africa, Asia, India, Gypsies. This leads me to believe that ol' "E Pluribus Unum" has been around.

Ask a Christian about sin and he will tell you that everybody has sinned. He will claim that everybody was born in (into, with) sin. These prepositions are very tricky. Try this for instance: the dog is barking in the hall. Does that mean the dog is in the hall? Are souls in babies the moment that conception takes place? Do souls enter the fetus and embryo? Are souls placed in the babies at the moment of birth?

What truly is the meaning of "sanctify"? What is the difference between the souls of the Rights and the souls of the Lefts? The Rights have the "gift," whether it be from God or Satan. I know this without knowing the mechanics of the transfer of souls.

Tennyson defined pantheism as the worship of objects in nature. Higher pantheism is that which identifies both nature and spirit.

Not long ago I went to see two "friends." There was a baby there. I patted the baby on the head, and for a split second I thought of killing the baby. I then sat down and glanced at the two "friends." They were both staring at me as if they knew the thought that had crossed my mind. They did know it, for somehow they had put it into my mind.

Not long ago a "friend" of mine and his very desirable wife came to see me. They are staunch Christians. He told me that they were going on a trip. Then, in an instant, I saw in my mind's eye a car wreck with him not there and his wife uninjured. I looked at him and he was staring at me as if he knew my thought. He did! He put it there!

Confessions of a Dandy

Through the years when I would be talking to Rights, they would say, "I've got a good picture of that." I assumed that they formed a picture in their minds from my words. This was not true. Somehow they can receive the picture that I form in my mind. I could give many examples of this occurring, but it will suffice to say it is fact.

There are several different kinds of intelligence. One theory states that the more intelligent a person is, the better he can adapt to changing environments. Another theory states that the more intelligent a person is, the better he is at deceiving and detecting deception. God is slowly giving me the gift of discernment of the spirits. I have seen Satan several times, and he looks like any other man. Each time I have known it was he.

I am not easily spooked. I can tell whether something in the environment is trying to spook me—TV, for instance. The TV Rights can give me a subliminal stimulus at a particular point in time, let's call it point A. My train of thought will logically go from point A to point B and, maybe, to point C. The time this thought process takes place is known. Science! Also known is the content which moves through time. When my mind arrives at point C or so, a great overt response comes on TV to match my thought at C.

While on the subject of TV, let us look at one program that has survived through the years: "The Andy Griffith Show." Barney is shown as a bumbling Left, and Andy the benevolent Right. The program is good entertainment for both the knowing Rights and the unknowing Lefts. I have noticed that there are muted responses (canned laughter) to inside jokes for Rights. It may lead you to wonder how much of your thought processes are truly your own, if any! Being a Left makes it difficult to understand the ease of the Rights in living in a dual world.

Freud said that almost all human behavior can be explained by an understanding of sex. Here are the different kinds of sexual behavior: (1) heterosexuality, (2) homosexuality, (3) bisexuality, (4) autosexuality, (5) asexuality, (6) group sex, and (7) sex with animals. Sex is so important because it is necessary for the propagation of the species. The soul itself is neuter. I have come to the conclusion that any sex other than for propagation is perverted. Since Rights control every other aspect of behavior by Lefts, I suspect that Rights control the sex habits of Lefts, too.

A girl I dated a few times practiced witchcraft. She went to South Carolina for a Satanic meeting, and when she returned she told me there were four hundred people there, drinking blood and cursing. She told me that my "bad luck" was the result of her witchcraft. About sixteen years ago she told me that when Jesus returned he would return to North Carolina.

Now let me mention the term *macho image*. This is a certain "air" of maleness that male Rights have about them from early manhood. Male Lefts do not have this because they are stuck in adolescence. They are called boys. Coleridge wrote: "For facts are valuable to a wise man chiefly as they lead to the discovery of the indwelling law. Which is the true being of things, the sole solution of their modes of existence and in the knowledge of which consists our dignity and our power." God is gradually giving me a macho image of my own.

As I mentioned, taking a dose of angel dust will put a person in tribulation for three days. When my "friend" slipped me some, I left his house and went home. Three days later he came to my house, and about fifteen minutes before he arrived I immediately came out of tribulation. When he arrived, he told me that about fifteen minutes earlier he had started to pray for me. The truth is, that was the point in time when he quit praying for me (to Satan). Other people are praying for me, but they don't represent God, either, although maybe a very few do.

I don't want to beat a dead horse, but I will say that my "friends" have "thrown me in the river" many times. To be truthful, I don't have any friends. I have "friends," but no friends.

A "friend" of mine in college, a Right to whom I had just told a lie—because I did not think he would believe the truth—said to another student, "I like to catch them [Lefts] in a lie and watch 'em squirm." Sometimes Rights will ask questions of Lefts when they already know the correct answers. It is a sport for Rights just to see what the Lefts come up with.

It might be mentioned here that there is plenty of contention between Rights. Most all famous people are Rights, and among them they are not of one accord, even though they may share the same spirit.

Madison Avenue gives substance to Freud's theory on sex. The Madison Avenue people know that sex can sell most anything. They cram subliminal sex into just about every advertisement.

Politics is known as the second oldest profession.

When I was teaching, there was a teacher who carried a handkerchief (I did not carry one.) Sometimes when I talked to him he would pull it out and sort of wave it in front of me while staring at my face. I don't know what response he was trying to elicit.

The ratio of Rights to Lefts on this planet is unknown to me. There were about thirty Satanists that I knew of out of about a thousand students in the school where I taught. That comes to about three percent. The Satanists are Rights; the Christians are also Rights. Many who consider themselves Christians are Lefts, but they don't know they are Lefts. The Rights know it, however. Some Satanists are active in the Christian Church.

The Baptists did a survey several years ago concerning the number of Baptists who were "born again." The study showed that only seventeen percent of their membership were "born again." Whether this study is indicative of the percentage of Rights to Lefts, I do not know. However, the Rights know. There are many Rights who are neither Christians, Satanists, nor followers of other religions.

For parameters of behavior in the spirit world, let us look at a particular event that occurred before my tribulation. Surly and I were in the pool room alone. He said, "I spent my money and I can't get my food stamps." I asked him how much money he needed. He replied, "Thirty-five dollars." I immediately gave him the $35 and he quickly put it in his pocket. Then he craned his neck and head around and looked intently as if he had broken a rule. I am sure that he influenced me to give him the money.

Let us look at a few more instances. Suppose I, a Left, run over a dog that belongs to a Right. I did not exactly do it on purpose, but I could have acted to avoid running over it. The dog was hit but not injured. Now this gives the Right a reason to run over my dog. This almost happened. A Right tried to run over my dog. I was very angry at this, but I thought awhile and made the connection.

In the second case, I got into a fight with a man, a Right who was very big and strong. He had a reputation of being mean as hell. I threw him down, then let him up. He punched me in the nose and knocked me down. He grabbed me by my hair. He could have injured me, maybe killed me, but instead he let me up. Now, I was not the least bit angered at this man. Maybe that is why he did not beat me up, maybe he couldn't.

Another time, a Right was mad at me. I had dated his wife before they were married, but I did not know this at the time. He kept picking on me, and I became very mad. I asked him to step outside. I beat him severely. The only thing that stopped me was his friend, another Right, cutting me with a knife.

In these two examples, the one you expect to have mercy—a Left, me—had no mercy. The one you would not expect to have mercy—a mean Right—had mercy. A week after I beat up the Right, he shot a man and killed him. He spent a very short time in prison, so I presume his victim had been a Left.

I joined a Church several years ago and attended regularly. There was an elderly lady who sat behind me. She would always raise her arms and hands in a certain manner. She was cool toward me. Suddenly I made a connection. I had seen that posture before by a Satan who was about to sacrifice me. The more I learn about Christianity and Satanism, the more they seem to have in common—in fact, the more all religions have in common.

A few years ago a "friend" of mine and I went to see a terminally ill "friend." I marveled at how well he took imminent death. Evidently Rights can make this transition very well.

One day I was at the hair stylist getting a haircut. I started a conversation with a middle aged woman in the barber chair. As she was leaving, I told her, "You would understand if you knew my mother." She glanced at me with a faint smile, which told me more than words could express. Ol' "E Pluribus Unum" really gets around.

Blackie owned a bar in town. He was microphobic (extraordinarily fearful of germs). He was constantly wiping the bar with alcohol. A "friend" of mine said I was one of those "two-wipe people." He told me that for people like me, Blackie wiped the bar twice. Evidently Blackie thought that Lefts are inherently dirtier than Rights. After giving some thought to this, I see that there may be some truth in it.

Socializing as an adult, I have been addressed by very few people by my first name. They usually make a statement with an implied "you." Sometimes they address me by my last name (very impersonal).

I have noticed that when I am unconscious about my body positions, I am very clumsy. I am always tripping over things, bumping into things. The Rights are very efficient in their movements because they have a better sense of body position. Most of the "bad luck" that Lefts have is initiated by some Rights. In a metaphorical sense, the Rights trip the Lefts and then punish them for being on the ground.

Why do Japanese students score significantly higher on intelligence tests than American students? One theory on intelligence is that mental capacity (the brain) is inherited. I asked a Japanese doctor why the Japanese people score so high on I.Q. tests. I asked him if the reason for this was heredity. He said that he would like to think so, but that it is not the case. The doctor said the reason for this is the highly structured life to which Japanese children are subjected. Is it that the ratio of Rights to Lefts is greater in Japan than in the U.S.? There may be some substance to this, but I don't know.

A "friend" of mine, a Right who is very intelligent, took the same intelligence test I did, and I scored higher than he did. In the classroom, however, he did much better than I did. I believe I was a victim of "Attention Deficit Syndrome," turned off and on at will by the Rights.

As I have mentioned before, a very old man, Amil, told me that in a few years there would be places to put people like me—Lefts. In Japan, people are closer to this than in the U.S. First of all, in Japan the Lefts are made to feel inferior. They are called "the unfortunate ones." They are given menial jobs that require little more mental effort than breathing. The Rights' control over the emotions of the Lefts may not have much bearing on the accumulation of facts. This is why the gifts that the Rights have may not help them very much while taking intelligence tests.

I am an unusual bird, a Left with a high I.Q. Until a few years ago, I always craved to be around people. Now I like to be alone. My mother says, "When you are alone, you are in good company." But how alone am I? Sitting here in my room alone, writing this paper, am I truly alone? I know that I am sending out brain waves. I know that brain waves are electrical; they are similar to radio waves. I could be alone and still easily be monitored.

Let me write something about slavery. Physical slavery is not true slavery. Mental slavery is true slavery. The Emancipation Proclamation is a joke. I would much prefer being a physical slave and mentally free than the other way around. The United States is loaded with mental slaves. I call them Lefts. I am one of them.

From the time I was about seven years old, my father required me to attend church every time the door opened: Sunday morning, Sunday night, Wednesday night. I was subjected to this until I was seventeen. I could not understand this "born again" and "Jesus loves me." One time some "friends" and I camped out deep in the woods on Saturday night. I was hoping to escape going to church. My father found me and forced me to attend church. Somehow he was receiving something out of this situation that I still don't understand. I sat beside him in church year after year, having no idea what was going on. The Rights did.

The Rights have excellent control over their emotions. They can match their facial expressions with any emotion they wish. These include fear, anger, attention, excitement, joy, sadness, and guilt. By controlling their facial expressions, they can induce the response they desire from Lefts.

When I am introducing one Right to another Right, they shut my brain down so that I forget both of their names, causing great embarrassment. There is a term that fits this type of activity: stumbling block.

This section ends with an English lesson. Blake, in "The Little Black Boy," penned the line, "I am black but O! My soul is white." Either some Rights have white souls and other Rights have black souls, or the white and black souls of the Rights are interchangeable. Browning wrote, "For one of faith diversified by doubt: We call the chess board white, we call it black." Does the chess board represent the universe of all souls, where the Rights are white and the Lefts are black? Or does the chess board represent the universe of all souls of only the Rights—the white representing the Christians and such, and the black representing the Satanists and such.

Here are other thoughts on the subject:

ROUSSEAU—"We must learn to trust the human heart as a guide to human action since emotion and natural instinct prompt wiser conduct than does reason."

WORDSWORTH—"The soul that rises with us our life's star, hath had elsewhere its setting and cometh from afar. But trailing clouds of glory do we come. From God, who is our home." And again, "Of sense and outward things, falling from us vanishing."

SHELLEY—"Depart not lest the grave should be, like life and fear, a dark reality." And, "Let me not vex with inharmonious sighs, the silence of that heart's accepted sacrifice."

TENNYSON—"For some three suns to store and hoard myself." And, "Who throve and branched from clime to clime, the herald of a higher race, and of himself in higher place, if so he typed this work of time."

DONNE—"Ask for those kings whom thou saw'st yesterday, and thou shalt hear, all in one bed lay." And, "Such wilt thou be to me, who must like the other foot, obliquely run: thy firmness makes my circle just, and makes me end, where I begun."

BAUDELAIRE—"Where in full day the spectre walks and speaks. These Centenarian twins, these spectres odd [seven times] these seven old hideous monsters had the mien of being immortal."

BROWNING—"Such feasting ended, then as sure an end to men." And, "Rejoice, we are allied with that which doeth provide."

And again, "But you were living before that, and also you are living after."

INGELOW–"I am old! You may trust me. I am seven times one today."

BLAKE (to his genius)–"Which is the Holy Ghost in man, there is no other." [Webster's Dictionary defines demon as "genius."]

BROWNING–"O thou soul of my soul! I shall clasp thee again, and with God be the rest!" And, "Why lose this life: The meantime since its use, may be to make the next life more intense." [Karma.]

Almost all of the writings of English literature can be understood with a knowledge of these two concepts: (1) "one among many" and (2) reincarnation. These concepts are expressed with several literary devices, mainly, extended metaphors, dichotomies, and allegories.

Frequent words English writers use in referring to these concepts are birth, life, death, the seasons, sleep, awake, spring, summer, fall, winter, the sun, the son, the daughter, the moon, the stars, days, nights, hell, heaven, heart, twilight, dawn, weeks, months, years, sky, sea, soul, glory, eternity, father, mother, sister, brother, love, hate, and all human emotions and experiences.

What is amazing about English writers is their ability to express the human experience in such numerous and creative ways. I am an unusual bird, indeed. I understand almost all of English literature. Once you have a grasp of the concepts of "one among many" and reincarnation, it all falls into place. Not only does English literature fall into place, but also contemporary life.

Part 7

Sol and Potpourri

SOLOMON (Psalm 8)–"O Lord our Lord, how excellent is thy name in all the earth! Who hast set thy Glory above the Heavens."

WORDSWORTH–"Thou dost preserve the stars from wrong; And most ancient heavens, through thee, are fresh and strong."

BURNS–"Give me a spark O' nature's fire, that's A' the learning I desire."

POPE–"Unerring nature, still divinely bright, One clear, unchained, and universal light."

BYRON–"To mingle with the universe, and feel What I can ne'er express, yet cannot all conceal."

DONNE–"To warm the world, that's done in warming us."

BAUDELAIRE–"Drawing the sun out of my heart and there with burning thoughts making a summer air."

VOLTAIRE–"Whatever is, is Right." And, "God has ordained the powers that be."

POPE–"To err is human, to forgive divine." And, "This is a day that the Lord has made." A reference to the sun?

BYRON (referring to Rights)–"Eternal spirit of chainless mind, bright in dungeons and liberty."

DANTE–"Limbus Patrum—from this, the souls predestined to salvation." Sanctified?

EMERSON–"Here we meet two familiar romantic and transcendental tenets: the divinity of nature and the brotherhood which man shares with man and with nature. . . . One item in nature to another, is more important than the individual item." A synergistic effect.

The sun, or our day-star, is a rather ordinary star. It has a diameter of 864,000 miles and is a mean 93 million miles from the earth. Our sun is a rather ordinary star in a rather ordinary galaxy, the Milky Way. All of the stars that you can see at night with the unaided eye are in the Milky Way. The Milky Way itself is in a cluster of neighboring galaxies. Andromeda is a sister to the Milky Way. Each of these galaxies contains about two billion stars. And consider this: there are billions of galaxies in the known universe. If that doesn't kill your pride, nothing will.

Our sun has been worshipped by all cultures from antiquity. There can be no doubt that all life depends on the energy from the sun. The ancients realized this and, therefore, worshipped the sun as a god. The huge physical structures of the ancient world were built for the sun god—Stonehenge, the Sphinx, the Easter Island heads, the pyramids.

The process by which the sun derives its energy is known. It is called fusion. Fusion occurs when two special types of hydrogen atoms, called deuterium, fuse. The result of this is the formation of a helium atom with less mass than the two hydrogen atoms that formed it. The lost mass is turned into energy. There are other atomic processes happening in the sun, but this is the most important. Scientists know how matter is changed into energy, but it is unknown how, or if, energy is changed into matter (steady state theory).

Why shouldn't modern man worship the sun? Modern man is every bit as dependent on the sun as ancient man was. Consider these:

Ecclesiastes 11:7–"Truly the light is sweet, and a pleasant thing it is for the eyes to behold the sun."

Jeremiah 15:9–"She [who] hath borne seven languisheth: She hath given up the ghost; the sun has gone down while it was yet day."

Joel 3:15–"The sun and moon shall be darkened."

Confessions of a Dandy

Malachi 4:2–"But unto you that fear my name shall the sun of righteousness arise with healing in his wings."

There are many theories about how life originated on this earth. One in particular fascinates me. It is the panspermal theory, which states that several billion years ago, when the solar system was young, an asteroid from beyond the solar system crashed onto the surface of the earth. With it came microbes which evolved over billions of years into our present day life forms.

What about the spirits? Where did they come from? It is a good bet that they came from outer space. Can they travel faster than the speed of light? Or can they travel as fast as the speed of light? It is my bet that the spirit(s) came to this earth about 8,000 years ago, giving certain people a "gift." The anatomy of the modern man was developed by that time. This "gift" enabled the people who possessed it to have an advantage over their fellow men. They could also have the knowledge to build ancient structures such as the pyramids.

A leading theory today is that man developed mental [spiritual] telepathy before he developed language. This is likely because of the vast number of people in the modern world who possess this "gift."

There are several references in the Bible concerning the sun's being darkened. Recently, I was driving east on Highway 54 at about noon. It had been a partly cloudy day, but at that period it was quite bright. Suddenly it became very dark. I turned on my headlights. The cars that I was meeting had on their headlights, too. Who has the power to turn the sun off and on?

The remainder of this section will have no particular structure, only events that I have observed.

There is an obscure theory of human behavior called "the sign post theory" (originated by Tolston, I believe). This theory states that we are enslaved by our environment. At every moment, our five senses take in stimuli. The strongest stimulus or combinations of stimuli will win the response. The response could be induced thoughts.

Knowing this theory—and it seems sound—it is easy to realize how a computer that can process a billion bits per second can control people (Big Brother).

Tennyson wrote, "I am part of all that I have met." Browning wrote, ". . . that low man goes on adding one to one. His hundred's soon hit: This high man, aiming at a million, misses an unit [himself]." The "gift" given by the spirit can enable these Rights to discern, in most cases, whether Lefts are telling the truth.

About seven years ago I went to the oral surgery department at U.N.C. Dental School. The doctor wanted to do a biopsy on my mouth. After taking the specimen, he told me to come back in a week and he would give me the results. A week later, when I returned, I was placed in a chair in a little room about ten feet by eight feet. A strange thing happened next. The little room became crammed full of little nurses and little student nurses. There must have been a dozen. Then the doctor came in and told me that I had pre-cancer and that if I didn't quit smoking I would die. A funny feeling came over me. I now realize why those little nurses were present. They were there to monitor the vibrations that I sent out when the doctor told me that I might die.

There must be an almost infinite number of emotions or feelings. Several times Rights have asked me, "Why don't you date [so-and-so—a woman much older than myself]?" I would reply, "She is too old." Then the Rights would laugh as if my reply was very funny.

How about the Liberty Bell? The Liberty Bell symbolizes freedom for the Rights. The crack symbolizes slavery for the Lefts. The Rights have eternal life. The Lefts do not have eternal life. I wonder how well the Rights could function if they had the same future as the Lefts, and knew it.

Now for good and evil. The original evil took place in the garden of Eden when Adam and Eve disobeyed God. Evil is anything that is not good, a rather gray definition. The Christians believe that people are born into sin. They believe that people are sinners from birth. I believe that babies are innocent at birth, that the concepts of good and evil are learned. The age at which these concepts are learned is probably earlier for Rights than Lefts. The age of accountability varies between the Rights and Lefts. The Rights develop these concepts much earlier than the Lefts because they have history on their side.

Also, I might mention proxy. Rights in particular have the ability to induce a feeling of elation and other emotions in Lefts. In doing this they get a sense of pleasure. Their pleasure is vicarious. Lefts may try this on Rights, but it doesn't work. It leaves Lefts with an empty feeling.

Let me mention tattoos. I always believed that people who had tattoos were dissatisfied with their bodies, and that they were ruining their bodies. The truth is, they think that with the right tattoos they can improve on nature. They are true expressionists.

There have been numerous instances when I was in the presence of groups of people who, I thought, were cursing other

Confessions of a Dandy

people. How naive I was. These people (Rights) were cursing me! I do not say this out of paranoia; I cannot be paranoid, because I have no fear. It is a little sad. Some of these people I liked.

How about some medicine? For fifteen years I took Prolyxin and Thorizen, two powerful anti-psychotic drugs. My body would literally vibrate when I went to bed, and I would fall asleep through pure exhaustion. Three years ago I was put on a new drug called Clozaril. I do not know the pharmacology of this drug, but I do know that I am very much improved. Mentally I am much better than I was before I experienced my breakdown. I am receiving insights that allow me to understand the world. I don't think I need to take any medicine now, but I must continue it in order to receive support.

A year ago I went on a short trip with my father in my car. I was driving, and we were listening to the radio. The road was unfamiliar and I was tense, following a pickup truck pulling a flatbed trailer with no brake lights. My father told me to tune in a certain station on the radio. I replied that I did not want to take my eyes off the road. A moment later the truck driver slammed on his brakes and I almost hit the trailer. I told my father that if I had been tuning the radio, we would have crashed. My father replied, "I made a mistake, I made a mistake." The mistake that he made was that the radio-tuning ploy did not cause me to hit that trailer.

One day I was at a pharmacy getting some medicine. I knew the correct prices of the medicine, so when I was about to pay my bill I discovered that I had been overcharged by ten dollars. I brought this mistake to the attention of the pharmacist and she said, "I made a mistake, I made a mistake." Her mistake was getting caught!

Above all, there are only two emotions that can do me in: aggression and fear. The aggression is easy to cope with. I have never been an aggressive person. To handle fear is a little more difficult. I cope with fear with this thought: *if God wants me dead, there is nothing I can do to prevent my death.* Why worry? On the other hand, if God wants me to live, there is no force in the universe that can destroy me, including the devil. He has tried it many times.

Another characteristic that I (a Left) had was the giving away, to a Right—or lending to a Right, which is the same thing— anything that I possessed. I would even give away property that was not mine. This was a feeble attempt to make friendship. I thought that the more I gave people, the more they would like me. The opposite is true.

The Rights can con the Lefts into almost anything: lending money, for instance. All the Rights must do is persevere, and they will get the prize. They have no intention of paying it back. This goes for other property also.

Now let us look at the races of men (*Homo sapiens*). The scientific name of men, *Homo sapiens*, means wise man. All men are of the same species. The criterion that determines this is the ability of the races to crossbreed and produce fertile offspring. The races of men are all subspecies.

Subspecies are groups within a species—races, for humans—with some genetic differences. There are thirty-six shades of skin color, ranging from pure white to black, with each resulting from a special combination of genes. There are also genetic differences between the races in the other organ systems. This is why organ transplants between the races are seldom successful. I do not know the correlation of Rights to Lefts as far as races are concerned. There are Rights and Lefts in all races.

More about my experiences in the U.S. Army. After boot camp, I was sent to radar school at Fort Bliss, Texas. One morning I was running late and I was afraid I would miss formation (a real no-no in the army). I didn't have time to shave. One of the soldiers told the first sergeant that I hadn't shaved. The first sergeant sent me to get my razor and made me dry shave in front of the troops.

Two weeks later the same sort of thing happened. This time I did not have time to shower. This time the first sergeant said that I was going to get an Article 15 (punishment). I did not know what was happening to me. I wanted very much to be a good soldier. I now realize that the Rights were behind it all. They can easily cause a person not to shave or shower if that person is a Left. Indeed, the Rights trip the Lefts and then punish them for being on the ground.

Now let us examine cognitive and moral development. Cognitive development and moral development have almost no correlation to each other, but there is some correlation between a person's sex life and his cognitive development. One study revealed that the more intelligent a person, the more unusual his sex life.

The stages of moral development (Kohlberg) are as follows:

Level:
    I. Moral value is defined by punishment and reward.
        1. Obedience to rules and authority to avoid punishment.
        2. Conformity to obtain rewards and to exchange favors.

    II. Moral value resides in fulfilling the correct roles, in maintaining order and meeting the expectations of others.
        3. Conformity to avoid rejection by others.
        4. Duty, law, order.

III. Moral value resides in conformity; shared standards, rights, duties.
    5. Legalistic orientation, recognition of value of common good.
    6. Universal principal of right and justice.

Only fifty percent of people make it past level four (duty, law and order), and these people are mostly Rights. They have the spiritual equipment to fit into the universe.

The stages of cognitive development are as follows:

I. Sensory Motor, zero-eighteen months
    1. Preverbal
    2. Practical experiences
    3. Objects exist only in perceptual field.
II. Preoperational, eighteen months to seven or eight years
    1. Trial and error thinking
    2. Confuses number with size and shape.
    3. Thought concrete
    4. Cannot put himself in other's place.
III. Concrete operations, seven-eight to eleven-twelve years
    1. Thought processes concrete
    2. Serial
    3. Classification
    4. Conservation
    5. Concept of reversibility

The absence of a correlation between cognitive development and moral development—equating morals with the law—explains why some criminals are very intelligent. Some very intelligent people put a premium on high intelligence. Blake, for instance, showed himself to be in that category when he wrote that he did not care whether a man was good or evil but whether he was wise.

The Satanic Bible says, "Cursed is he who doeth good unto others who sneer upon him in return, for he shall be despised." I can relate to that verse. Another idea to which I can relate in the Satanic Bible is the teaching against allowing "psychic leaches" to use the Satanists. "Psychic leaches" are mostly Lefts. I have found that I have been a "psychic leach" to many Rights during my life.

In 2 Corinthians 11:12 we read, "But what I do, that I will do, that I may cut off occasion from them which desire occasion; that wherein they glory, they may be found even as we." Wordsworth wrote, "Oh! Confidence misplaced." Rights allow Lefts to lean on them to varying degrees. It gives Lefts a feeling of security if the

Rights allow them to "lean" on them, regardless of how false it really is.

After my tribulation I was desperate for someone to lean on. I made friends with a retired teacher who was about my age. I went over to his house several times. We went fishing once. I thought the guy had a loose screw, and I could never feel comfortable in his presence. He would not let me become a "psychic leech." He would say things, do things, and put out vibrations to make me feel insecure. I did not know this at the time, but I know it now.

Some Rights use their spiritual gifts to their advantage, to the misfortune of Lefts. Lefts can never accumulate any wealth because of the spiritual power of the Rights. The Rights can talk the Lefts into almost anything they wish.

What about the evolutionary aspects of the spiritual world? I suspect that the Rights are gradually crowding out the Lefts. Even if the Rights have no biological descendants, they can still have spiritual descendants. As for myself, my mother did not raise me to be a father or a husband. She told me many times that she did not want any grandchildren. My feelings counted less than zero. She probably has her spiritual life sanctified.

All that I am left with is God!

PART 8

A Dandy's Plight

I would like to tell the story of a dandy, Beau Brummell. He was born in England in 1778 and died in France in 1840. The most obvious feature of a dandy is his elaborate dress. For several years Beau was at the pinnacle of London's social life. Even Byron showed him respect. For a while he was consul at Caen, but soon lost the post in the course of his rapid deterioration. He became heavily in debt from gambling and went to France to escape his creditors.

The powerful friends who had supported him died or withdrew their support. His health gradually deteriorated, and he was forced to sell his prize possession, his snuff box. He died at the charitable asylum of Bon Sauveur. Beau had deteriorated in every sense of the word. The life of some dandies can be described as an extended "flash in the pan." It ends in death.

In Matthew 5:13 it is written, "Ye are the salt of the earth; but if the salt have lost its savour, wherewith shall it be salted? It is thenceforth good for nothing, but to be cast out, and to be trodden under foot of men."

As I have mentioned earlier, I had a run-in with some Satanists—one in particular. I was trapped at his house with other Satanists present. This one particular Satan I shall call Silly. Silly jumped up and down and yelled that he was God. Then he jumped up and down and said that he was Satan. Then he became calm and looked at me. His mouth flew open and he had a look of fear, and he asked, "Are you him?" And then he said, "No you couldn't be, you're not old enough." Silly then declared, "I am God, and I have the power of life . . ."—he pointed to his baby—"and death"—and he pointed at me. He added, "Why don't you get it over all at once instead of dying a little at a time"?

Upon examination of the motives of the Christians and the Satanists I must conclude that they are similar. The Satanists desire to kill the non-spiritual people (Lefts, men). On the other hand, the Christians are willing to wait for the death of Lefts by natural causes—accident, suicide, and occasional murder. Amen.

The difference is time. Christians have eternal spirit; Satanists have eternal flesh. Both hate men. Like Beau Brummell, I am a dandy, but, by the grace of God, I will not be a flash in the pan.

PAPER TWO
Little Timmy

Much has been written about the author Virginia Woolf (1882-1941), English novelist, short story writer, biographer, and essayist. One of her major achievements was her development of the stream-of-consciousness technique. Her biography of Beau Brummell (1778-1849) is her best known work. Although the word dandy is not mentioned, it can be inferred by the reader. Beau Brummell was, undoubtedly, a dandy. He was also a Left.

PART 1

In Search of the Dandy

Now we come to some heavy stuff: *Who's Afraid of Virginia Woolf?* The three acts in this play by Edward Albee are titled "Fun and Games," "Walpurgisnacht," and "The Exorcism." This play can be fully understood only by Rights—and only very intelligent Rights . . . well educated, intelligent Rights. Some of the play is in Latin.

There are only four players: Martha, fifty-two, George, forty-six, Honey, twenty-six, and Nick, thirty. All of the play takes place in the apartment of George and his wife, Martha. Martha is the daughter of the president of the college where George is a history professor.

As the play opens, George and Martha are waiting for Nick, a new biology professor, and his wife, Honey, to arrive. When Nick and Honey get there, they all start drinking. They drink all night long. Much of this play is occupied with light banter—a highly intellectualized banter.

Why would anybody be afraid of Virginia Woolf? Is it her expertise on dandies? I think so; I believe that is it. Several times during the play Martha and George sing "Who's Afraid of Virginia Woolf?" (to the tune of "Who's Afraid of The Big Bad Wolf?"). At the end of the play, Martha admits that she is afraid of Woolf.

All four of the characters are well past tipsy when George mentions his and Martha's teenage son, who had been killed in a car wreck. She is furious at George for bringing up the subject after he had promised not to. Martha blurts out, "You killed him, George."

Now, where does the dandy fit in? Realizing that the deceased son was a dandy is the only way that the play makes any sense. This opens a Pandora's box of questions. Why would two very intelligent Rights have a dandy for a son? How did George take part in killing their son? The ol' E Pluribus Unum makes George the culprit.

My parents are intelligent Rights. Why would they have a dandy—me!—for a son? Poe writes, "Can it be fancied that deity ever vindictively made in his image a mannikin merely to madden it?"

There is a bridge near my house. Two times I almost hit the bridge and one time I did hit it. On each of those occasions I was returning from a party. I was not drunk and only a little bit sleepy. Why did I lose consciousness at that particular place three times in a row—the most dangerous place on my travel home? I could be nice and blame it on the devil, but I will blame it on E Pluribus Unum.

What is the relationship between E Pluribus Unum and the devil? Are dandies created only to be sacrificed? These are questions that I cannot answer, but I have all the confidence in the world that God will reveal the answers to me in due time. I believe I will receive these revelations as I write these papers. As I write, I know that my mind is being monitored by Rights. This monitoring does not break the spiritual-physical boundary, although these papers do break the spiritual-physical boundary. How extensively my thought processes can be used against me I do not know.

God has let me know that I must receive absolutely no pleasure from the misfortune of others. It must not even enter my mind; and it doesn't. I played poker for many years. My reason for playing was fellowship. I thought this was the reason other players played also. How naive I was.

I know the Bible states that the love of money is the root of all evil, but I'll go one step further: money itself is the root of all evil. There is some intrinsic property of money that leads people to behave very strangely. It must be understood that man is a value-creating animal.

In Dante's *Inferno*, the fourth circle of hell is occupied by hoarders and spendthrifts.

When Love is Given/Love is Heaven.
When Love is Lent/Love is Spent.
When Love is Sold/Love is Cold.
When Love is Bought/Love is Naught.

One year when I was teaching school, I had grown a beautiful salad patch. My mother picked two bags full of salad, one for the principal and one for the secretary. When I gave the secretary her bag, she said, "What really matters is that you picked them." A funny feeling came over me.

LYTTON–"There's no weapon that slays its victim so surely (if well aimed) as praise."

Here is a statement by Conrad. I do not know what to make of it–"Supernatural source of evil is not necessary. Men alone are quite capable of every wickedness." Is the human *race* a verb or a noun?

It is said that the pen is mightier than the sword. How can this be? The pen represents thoughts, the sword represents the physical. Thoughts control the physical.

How can Rights know the future? I know for a fact that some of my "friends" knew that I was going to be killed by a train years before it almost happened. That incident leads me to question whether time is truly a linear function.

American Indians have always been of interest to me. The Indians have been treated terribly through the years. Union General Philip Sheridan, for whom my grandfather was named, declared, "The only good Indians I ever saw were dead." A related quote from Kilby reads, "I want that crude hard-fisted tale where seven more redskins bit the dust."

There is little doubt that the Indians migrated from Siberia to Alaska during the Pleistocene era. From Alaska they migrated to all of North, Central, and South America. Blood-typing studies on these Indians show that there were at least two separate migrations.

Some years ago a little Indian boy lived in my grandfather's rental house. The boy was not allowed to attend school. I could not understand this.

One summer I camped out at Smokemount, a national park in the Smokey Mountains. I attended a ranger's lecture about the mountains. I could not believe what I heard. The ranger quite openly expressed hatred for the Indians. What about the baloney "Great White Father in Washington?" Indians were referred to as savages. The real savages were the white people. I very much suspect that Indians are dandies. That is the only conclusion that I can come to. Truth does not need to be defended.

After taking a personality test in college, I had an appointment with the psychologist. He told me that my strongest trait was loyalty. This is why the truth is so hard on me. I am fooled by no one. Motives—ulterior motives—forget it. I understand.

Here is what is really sad: the property of being a good Christian is being a good deceiver. Butler–"The best liar is he who makes the smallest amount of lying go the longest way." The Bible teaches against praying in public like the Pharisees. I have been to a Gideon Prayer Breakfast and it is much like a contest to see who can out-pray the others. When Ricky Nelson was killed in a plane crash several years ago, a Gideon said, "Well, we got rid of another one."

A Christian who read my papers said that my paranoia shows through in them. What is paranoia? Irrational fear? What is the difference between rational fear and irrational fear? I believe there is a very large gray area between the two. I know there are several people who desire to kill me. Am I paranoid? What if I do not fear them? Rational or irrational?

When someone gives me praise, I know it is phony. I receive my reinforcement inadvertently from the Rights. I am much more aware of the scope of things than one can imagine.

Now let me state this about creeds: there are truly only two creeds, the Rights and the Lefts.

TENNYSON–"Who keeps the keys of all the creeds?"

GIBBONS (1810-1892)–"We are coming Father Abraham, three hundred thousand more." Civil War?

WORDSWORTH–"Creeds grow so thick along the way, their boughs hide God."

I realized many years ago that there were two types of jokes: a "shop" joke and a "spontaneous" joke. A little man told me, "I met a pretty girl down on one of those South Sea islands. What's the name of the island? I can't think of it." I responded, "Jamaica?" He replied "No, I didn't even kiss her." I marveled for many years about that joke, wondering why I had thought of Jamaica of all the South Sea islands, thus, setting up the punch line. I didn't realize that he had put it in my head.

Caverley states, "As the flight of a bird in the air, is the flight of a joke." Wooden legs are not hereditary, wooden heads are.

Everybody at some time must take stock of his life to see if it is worthwhile. If the pluses outweigh the minuses, then life will go on. If the minuses outweigh the pluses, life will end. Suicide.

There is a love-hate relationship within ourselves. There is also a love-hate relationship with other people, those who are closest to us.

Now let's have a little college sports. For years I thought the purpose of sports was to give the fans something with which to identify. The games were to satisfy primitive urges. The urges were masochism (when their team was losing) and sadism (when their team was winning).

The ram Rameses is the mascot of the University of North Carolina. The ram is the universal symbol of sacrifice. Now this ram is named Rameses. Some of the Pharaohs' names were Rameses. The Rameseses of old were sun worshippers. What about the North Carolina nickname, Tarheels? The tar represents the Lefts, the heel represents the Rights. This "Tarheel" business also occurs at other schools. There are merely variations on the same theme.

In the yearbook of the school which I attended, there was a large picture of watermelon rinds. The caption stated, "Keep the good [Rights] and throw away the bad [Lefts]."

Perverseness is one of the primitive impulses of the heart. Some people who have the "gift" are just plain stupid. Of people, persons, and humans, only one term refers exclusively to mankind: persons.

Now let me mention two of the most fundamental concepts in human nature: hope and trust. Hope is the most fundamental concept of all. It is also the first concept formed during development. Without hope, we all die.

In Paper One, I mentioned Watts's painting of a young person bound and blindfolded on a globe of the world, saying that my grandfather had a copy of it hanging on his wall. He often pointed it out to me. The title of this popular picture, which was found on many calendars throughout the world, is "Hope." Does this picture represent the hope of the Rights? What about the Lefts? In my opinion, this is a very sick painting.

Several years ago my mother (an accomplished painter) painted a picture of a young black boy walking toward the end of a pier. He was wearing men's boots, much too big for him. The picture very much resembled me. In fact, one of my "friends" remarked on several occasions, "That picture looks like you." Is this my mother's concept of my hope?

Howe states, "We should not expect something for nothing, but we do. It is called hope."

Ecclesiastes 9:4—"To all the living there is hope."

Now about trust. Trust is almost as important a concept as hope. We learn at a very early age to trust our parents and other grownups around us. We have no choice. The Lefts are deceived to the hilt by this early trust. Later in life they are betrayed by this same trust. Faithfulness is rewarded with treachery. Wordsworth–"Oh! Confidence misplaced."

When I was very young I realized that I had the gift of abstract thought. It was by this gift that I created my own world to live in. An old lawyer made the statement, "Trust none among the living and walk softly among the dead."

RANDOM THOUGHTS

It amuses me to imagine that the Rights have created a "Frankenstein's monster" and they do not know what to do with it. They can't kill it, although they have tried dozens of times. One of the Rights' favorite tricks is to answer a question with a question. The big difference between Rights and me is that I can tell spiritual truths and they can not.

The Right-Left business must be true. It is the only way that things make sense. When I laugh at Barney on the Andy Griffith Show, I am aware that Barney plays a Left. I am laughing at myself. What is laughter? It is a response that tells other people, "Yes I can see the incongruity in a situation."

Until Christ returns, Satan rules. Is Jesus God? God saved me from hell.

Love is the test for divine life.

When I was sick, Christians rejected me.

A "friend" of mine could tell when the phone was going to ring before it rang. Tactile.

The Beatitudes and many other sayings in the Bible are no more than allegories, moral metaphors.

An old man told me, "There are two types of people, the caught and the uncaught." No one can stand justice.

BRONTE–"The human heart has hidden treasures, in secret kept, in silence sealed; the thoughts, the hopes, the dreams, the pleasures, whose charms were broken if revealed."

How about Neanderthal man? How about modern man? Some paleontologist believe that they were contemporaries. Neanderthal had a larger cranium than modern man (*Homo erectus*). That does not necessarily mean greater intelligence. What did in the Neanderthals was the spirit—or their lack thereof. Where did the spirit come from? Somewhere in the universe. It chose to enter modern man. With modern man in possession of this "gift," he made quick work of Neanderthal.

The pride of ancestry increases in the ratio of distance.

There is some method by which Rights can tell a Left not to do a certain thing and then cause that Left to do it. This is a perverted process used by Rights for entertainment. I believe that all humanity possess dignity, not just the self-righteous Rights. If there is any truth in the story of Dr. Jekyll and Mr. Hyde, it is that we all have God and Satan in ourselves.

Here is something that I have observed. Through the years I have been invited to many banquets, pig-pickings, and cook-outs. Tons of food were there. I ate like a bird. For some reason I was not hungry. Many more times I was hungry and there was no food. I invited a "friend" over to my house and I gave him a steak. He invited me over to his house and he gave me a stone.

When I was but a toddler, my mother would jump up and down in front of me and yell, "You hate me, you hate me!" This behavior upset me very much. I could not hate her because that emotion was not in my young psyche. I did not know what the term "hate" meant.

The more I reflect on my early childhood, the more I believe that I was the perfect baby. I will only say two more words about this subject: my family.

My memory is returning to me better than ever. If I call a phone number two or three times, I remember it. My brain is better at organizing signals. I can block out background signals at will, or bring them up to conscious level at will.

A few days after I escaped from being sacrificed, I was very frightened. I went to the Sheriff's Department for protection. I told the detective about some boys with whom I associated (and, incidentally, liked) stealing some things. I was not in my right mind or I would never have told on them. At any rate, the boys knew instantly that I had told on them. They knew this by spiritual means. They said they would get even with me, and they did. All they needed was a couple of deputies tuned in on the crooks' wave length.

Do not love the world or the things in the world.

Now let me mention names. Science uses the binomial system of nomenclature. This system is in Latin. Each organism has its own scientific name composed of the genus and species. This Latin name describes the most obvious characteristic of the organism. Latin is used for uniformity. The scientific name of man is *Homo sapiens*, wise man.

Now what about other names? Are they descriptive? Several years ago I was in the presence of two men, Lacy and Larry. Lacy said, "I'm a Lacy, and you are a Larry, but what's a Timmy?" The names described the physical traits of these two men to perfection. The question is still unanswered. What's a Timmy?

A big unanswered question to me is exactly how the Rights know whether Lefts are lying. I do not possess an understanding of this process now, but I am acquiring it.

Is an understanding of God like the three blind men feeling an elephant? Each one is sure that he is correct and that the others are wrong. Or is an understanding of God like comparing apples and oranges?

Just after my first tribulation I had a feeling of humility, which is a characteristic of my illness. I asked an old "friend" if I had been hard on people. He said that I had been hard on people through the years. At that point I began some soul searching which continues until today.

Many years ago, I was at a bar that was owned by a very crafty old man. I heard him make the statement, "During a transaction, a nigger can tell whether that transaction is correct, but he cannot tell why it is correct or not."

My lab partner in a physics class was a math major. She would solve very complex problems with her slide rule. I could tell whether the answer was correct. She marveled at this. I could not tell why the answer was or was not correct.

The human brain is very much like a computer. The brain cells (neurons) operate on what is known as the "all-or-none" principle; either the cells fire or they don't fire. Computers also operate on the "all-or-none" principle.

I will close with a bit of wit: the only thing that is worse than being talked about is not being talked about.

Grease it good and it works both ways.

PART 2

Biology

(The Study of Life)

Having been a biology teacher, I should be an expert on life. You be the judge. Will you defend my right to say what I believe, even though you disagree with it? I would do it for you.

There comes to my mind the fable about an old man who spent his whole life searching the world over for something that he never found. What was he looking for? An honest man.

The hardships I endured when I was growing up were very good training for the task that I am now performing. I am trying to make something rational out of this world.

I have discovered how to avoid having your secrets known: don't have any secrets.

If no person will tell the truth to me, then God will. The only one who has not betrayed me is God.

The dandy was meant to be sacrificed. This is the only way my life can be understood. The Rights are cursing me because God is showing me the truth, and the Rights cannot stand my knowing the truth. They consider me the devil because I am learning their Satanic secrets.

I am not at all ashamed of the papers that make up this book. Quite the contrary: I am proud of the truth. The only people that my papers make nervous are the ones who are afraid of the truth.

The Rights cannot deny the papers, because to do so is to acknowledge them. Salvation is a gift from God, not Satan.

What is the difference between looking *with* your eyes and looking *through* your eyes? If a person looks *through* his eyes, he becomes much more aware of the three-dimensional aspect of objects. There could be more.

Are the Rights at least part aliens? If you consider the spirit that entered man about eight thousand years ago as alien, then, the answer is yes. I am certain of this: any statement made to a Right is instantly known to all Rights. These papers included! E Pluribus Unum.

I have faith that the God of the dandy will prevail. How can the sins of the dandy be laid upon him when he is controlled by the Rights? The Rights must not only account for their own sins but for the sins of the dandies as well.

I thought people would help a person who was mentally ill in any way they could. Instead, they delight in torturing the mentally ill. Is this Christianity?

Where were the Christians

. . . when I was put in a straight jacket?

. . . when I was put in a padded cell?

. . . when I was strapped down in bed?

I must pretend to be interested in money. As long as I have the necessities for life and, maybe, a little money in my pocket, I am satisfied.

There are really only two creeds: the spiritual and the non-spiritual. Within the creed of the spirituals are many sub-creeds, which may also be termed creeds.

I am schizophrenic. Are all dandies schizophrenic? Are all schizophrenics dandies? My thought on this subject is that all dandies are, indeed, schizophrenic. My life is typical of the life of a schizophrenic, except that on my way to the bottom, God took alcohol away from me. I have been on my way up ever since.

There has been much hokum written about the lives of Rights—how much pain they go through, and how they suffer through all the different passions of mankind. The truth is they do not know what real pain is and do not want to know what real pain is. If you want to know what real pain is, ask a dandy.

Some of the Rights think I am the devil, but I *know* they are the devil. A Satanist I knew said that Satan was going to get me. At the time I did not believe Satan existed. I flatly told him, "Bullshit. I don't believe it." His chin dropped and he had a look of fear. He repeated several times "He is going to get you." That man is dead.

It is my idea that there are many Christians who do not profess to be Christians. I believe in the second coming of Christ. It was the religious leaders of two thousand years ago who crucified Christ. My contention is that the religious leaders of today are no different from the religious leaders of two thousand years ago. If the returning Christ does not fit their idea of the Messiah, they will reject him again—with a far different outcome.

Now for a little English language. What about the following compliment? "I think a lot of you." The term *lot* means a person's fate and worldly ways. Abraham's nephew was named Lot. His wife was turned into a pillar of salt. "Ye are the salt of the earth." Is all of this salt business aimed at the dandy?

The best term I can think of that describes the Christians is *smug*. Here is good advice for everybody: being aware of what you don't know is almost as important as knowing what you do know.

Many people truly believe that Satan is God and that God is Satan.

There are places in the Bible where God rewards deceit. One case in particular is that of Jacob and Esau. This is where the term "fleeced" originated. Why does God require us to live such moral lives when he approves of all sorts of treachery throughout the Bible? I believe the purpose of much Christian literature is to deceive the dandies.

Is there any connection between souls and spectres? It is my idea that the spectres are visible souls (spirits).

What about automatic writing? I didn't believe in automatic writing until I did it. I tried my best not to write, but I wrote anyway.

Many years ago, down at Silly's, he asked me if anyone knew I was there. "No," I replied. Later I realized that they were going to sacrifice me. That question, "Does anyone know you are down here?" should be like a red flag. Several times my "friends" have asked me that question, and only later did I understand that they were motivated to ask for the same reason that Silly had.

The Rights sometimes put pressure on me. Sometimes it is considerable and sometimes only a little. God has let me know that he will allow no more on me than I can stand.

Here is something that I wonder about. If Jesus was God, did he feel any physical pain when he was crucified?

I have discovered a new element in my psyche: notions, or impulses. Now instead of acting on a notion, I reflect on that notion and can sometimes identify the source.

I know some people who are both devoted Christians and devoted Shriners. How could this be? If indeed the Shriners are Satanic, these people are playing both ends against the middle. Are they worshipping two gods, or are they worshipping one God?

When I was in tribulation about fifteen years ago, I walked through the woods to a beautiful spring where I had played as a child. Someone had destroyed it. The spade marks were fresh, showing that it had been done recently. This was an act of Satan, not God.

Several years ago my nephew received a new gun for Christmas. He wanted to shoot something. I told him to put up some targets in the woods. He said no, that he wanted to shoot something alive. He shot three eastern turkey buzzards, which is a protected species. Is this urge to kill genetic or spiritual? Or both? Somehow such people as my nephew obtain pleasure from killing.

I could give numerous instances of Satan's destroying nature—not only nature, but the property of dandies as well. The devil loves death. Everybody has dignity, but Satan wants to take even the last bit of dignity from a person—his life.

I have always had the feeling of being an outsider. I thought I was the life of the party, but actually I was the laugh of the party. I wonder how it would be if this Right-Left thing were reversed. I have a feeling that the Rights can dish it out, but they can't take it.

Man will let you down every time, but God will never let you down. The dandy is content living with alms (minimum wage), but this is because of the world structure. Maybe a dandy is born a dandy, although I don't believe so. I believe a dandy becomes a dandy at about age two or three years, maybe earlier. Who is going to play God and make a child a dandy? Parents? God? Satan?

I cannot believe that God would do such a thing. That leaves parents and/or Satan. Evidently if you sell your soul to the devil, you do not go to hell. If you sell, or give, your soul to Christ, you do not go to hell. What is the difference?

Jesus said, "No man cometh to the father but by me." Does the word "man" preclude any dandies becoming Christians? I can forget about finding any dandies as old as I am, because there are none.

God is becoming tired of man thinking that he is God, and he is soon going to put a stop to it. He is also becoming tired of Satan impersonating him.

I do not desire to destroy Rights. Do they desire to destroy me? Are they mad or afraid of my writing? I'm supposed to be insane. If the Rights sacrifice people, they are working for the devil. This truth is self-evident.

Some young people, ten or twelve years old, are sometimes referred to as "old," as in old Joey or old Susan. They seem to have a certain air about them that is much older than their chronological age. This is because of the spirit, which is much older than the body. Some young people are wise beyond their years.

In the past, I used to laugh at fortune tellers. I don't exactly know the mechanics of how the fortune tellers receive their knowledge, but I know that it is a mysterious process. I know for a fact that some people can predict the future. Maybe some people can obtain information from that immortal sea to which both Satanists and Christians have access.

One Christian, a very intelligent person whom I have known all my life, read only two of my papers, One and Three. The morning after he had read them, I met him for breakfast. He was very nervous until I began the conversation, then he sighed with relief.

"I'm glad to hear you say that," he declared.

"Say what?" I asked.

"I'm glad to hear you say that you are not God," he replied.

The Rights are not dealing with little Timmy any longer, and they know it. God has a shield around me, and they know that also. They would much prefer dealing with little Timmy, for the new Timmy is spiritual.

Let me now write about the most truthful person in this country: Bill Cosby. Several years ago he entered a room while attending a party. There was a picture of Abraham Lincoln hanging in the room. Mr. Cosby took the picture off the wall and threw it to the floor and asked, "What has he ever done for us [black people]?" This was a declaration that the purpose of the Civil War was not to free black slaves. It is as obvious as the nose on your face.

If you desire to know more about dandies, read Virginia Woolf's *Beau Brummell*, about the most famous dandy of all (other than me).

There are many Rights who do not want to acknowledge my existence. They think if they hate me hard enough, I will disappear. It is much like the story of David and Goliath. I am David; guess who is Goliath. I sometimes wonder if my family has made a pact with the devil, but I am not at all sure of the answer.

Many Rights are sillies when it comes to dandies. This is something that I am beginning to notice. I am beginning to speak with authority, through no effort of my own. People cannot gainsay me as they did at one time. A dandy exhibits fierce individualism. It is obvious in his dress and his actions. There is just something about his air and the way he carries himself that is different from other people. The color and design of clothes remind me of certain people.

Years ago my college roommate said that his father told him this: "Never go to bed with a girl that you would not marry." I have often wished that my father had imparted that wisdom to me. It would have saved me many sorrows.

I will give you just one example of the inconveniences that befall a dandy. One day I received a statement from the doctor. It was incorrect. I went to the doctor's office the next day, but the secretary that handled such problems was not there. So I returned the following day. The secretary was too busy, and she asked me to return "tomorrow," which I did. I made three trips to the doctor's office, when I should not have had to make any. All of my transactions are similar to this.

Sometimes I think God is using me to torment the devil. Wisdom is dangerous to the Satanists.

Can it be that not telling certain people the truth is deceptive? I have a vague feeling that if I give a paper to a Right, all Rights know it. I have tried it time and time again, and I have proven that in some cases the Rights can see through my eyes. They somehow monitor the optic centers of the cerebrum.

Maybe hating dandies is spiritual. Maybe hating dandies is genetic. Maybe hating dandies is for survival of the fittest—both spiritual and physical. That is what Khrushev said; that is what a preacher said; that is what Darwin said.

I go to a Food Lion not far from where I live. I feel slight pressure most of the time when I enter the Food Lion. I feel as though I am a rat in a maze. What will stimulate me and cause me to buy a certain item? There are more rats in the store also, but I am the granddaddy of the rats.

My emotions—fear, anger, joy, guilt, sadness—are gradually leaving me. But I will never surrender love. I am becoming all things to all people. I am the worst teacher possible and the best teacher possible. My weaknesses are becoming my strengths.

Is the thought of doing something the same as doing it? I don't believe it. The thought of something is between the spiritual and the physical. There is a term that is used for this: poltergeist. However, Christ said that the thought of a sin is the same as doing it. Catch all.

God wants me to live; Satan wants me to die. Who do you think will prevail? I have no power at all except from God.

Here is a good piece of advice:

1 Corinthians 10:12–"Wherefore let him that thinketh he standeth take heed lest he fall."

Therefore modesty is very important.

Some one who is not modest runs the risk of becoming over-specialized. An organism in nature that becomes over specialized stands the risk of becoming extinct. Only a slight change in the environment could mean death.

Let me now write about the extremely subjective grading system at U.N.C. Graduate School. I attended a seminar at U.N.C.G. I was a dead duck the minute I walked in the door. Here we go with the dandy being abused again. Since I am a dandy, the professor thought I was inherently inferior. I could not change his mind. He gave me a C; the minimum grade that is accepted in graduate school is a B.

Maybe I will make a B on these papers.

In spite of knowing what I know, I still love my country. I am like an old dog whose master kicks him, but he stills loves his master.

If you think you are happy, then you are happy. What about a person who is a phony? He is the last person to realize that he is a phony—if he ever realizes it.

I am sure that Virginia Woolf did not plan for a dandy to read her biography of Beau Brummel and understand it. Most dandies are aloof and do not understand things. Why this is, I do not know.

Mom loves me with a passion and hates me at the same time. When I was growing up, I had first class treatment, physically. During this time I was subjected to mental abuse to the extreme. My mother tried to make me depend on her as much as possible. Also my mom tries to humiliate me, as if I have no dignity. Mom pulls things out of thin air and makes it seem of utmost importance. This behavior is typical of women. Mom also attempts to make me speak evil of certain people and speak good of others. She baits me, if you will, always needing to have something, such as chores, hanging over my head. I can do a few chores for Mom and start to retire for the night and invariably she will say, "I want you to do this and that in the morning."

Some scholars believe that the love a person receives as a child from his mother is the love that a person gives to his spouse, or anybody, for that matter. Being a dandy, I wonder about these things. Is my relationship with my mother typical of the mother-dandy relationship experienced by other dandies? I realize that my mother and I have an extremely bizarre relationship. Maybe it can be termed perverted. This leads me to wonder about the love (or whatever you call it) that I received from my mother. Compassion is hard on the truth.

This brings together two terms: loyalty and love. Love cannot be defined, only described. The term *loyal* means faithful to a cause. It has been shown to me that I am an extremely loyal person. This is one reason that these papers are so hard on me. I have been betrayed by my mother (who ruined my life completely), my family, my friends, and my associates.

The fact that the soul is neuter is written in many books, including the Bible. This is a touchy one for some Christians. I believe that Platonic love is the greatest love. Sexual love is no more than lust. Platonic love involves the meeting of the minds instead of a meeting of the bodies. Since the soul is neuter, the sex of an individual has nothing to do with Platonic love. Platonic love is on a higher plane: the intellect.

Some people attempt to make me feel insecure, but true security is not in the physical state; it is in the spiritual state.

I do not know how Mark Twain obtained the knowledge to write *Huckleberry Finn*, but I suspect that it was from a Satanic source. Very mysterious.

I mailed out many letters to publishing companies attempting to have these papers published, or at least proofread. For many months I received no response at all. I might be like Van Gogh. Van Gogh sold exactly one painting in his lifetime. Now his paintings are priceless. Three years ago one of his paintings sold for $33 million. When he was alive he could not give his paintings away. His brilliance was not realized until his death.

Ah, sweet mystery of life.

PART 3

The Master's Degree

Man's work is never done, either in this life or in any other. In this paper I attempt to make sense out of the English language. The terms with which I shall begin are: Lefts (non spiritual), Rights (spiritual), Man, Mankind, Men, Immortality, Sun, Son, one among many.

LEFT BASHING

Let us begin with men. Generally speaking, this term refers to Lefts, or non-spiritual people. English literature is not very kind to men who are non-spiritual. The context in which the term is used, as implied by the spiritual writer and inferred by the spiritual reader, means nothing to the non-spiritual reader.

The following are several references on how the Rights feel about the Lefts.

WHITTIER–"We seem to see our flag unfurled, our champion whiting in his place for the last battle of the world, The Armageddon of the Race."

HOLMES–"For there never was a pitcher that wouldn't spill, and there's always a flaw in a donkey's will."

LINCOLN–"Conceited whelp! We laugh at thee, nor mind that not a few of pompous, two-legged dogs there be conceited quite as you."

POE–"The play is the tragedy, 'man' and its hero the conqueror worm."

POE–"Can it be fancied that deity ever vindictively made in his image a mannikin merely to madden it?"

DICKENS–"Old Marley was as dead as a door-nail. . . the wisdom of our ancestors is in the simile," and "Let sleeping dogs lie."

BRONTE–"The human heart has hidden treasures, in secret kept, in silence sealed; the thoughts, the hopes, the dreams, the pleasures, whose charms were broken if revealed."

SHAW–"Better make a weak man your enemy than your friend."

LOWELL–"Slowly the bible of the race is writ, and not on paper leaves nor leaves of stone; each age, each kindred, adds a verse to it, texts of despair or hope, of joy or moan."

STORY–"I sing the hymn of the conquered, who fell in the battle of life; the hymn of the wounded, the beaten, who died overwhelmed in the strife."

WALLACE–"They say that man is mighty, he governs land and sea; he wields a mighty sceptre o'er lesser powers that be."

WHITMAN–"The real war will never get in the books."

INGELOW–"A land where all the men are stones, or all the stones were men."

BURTON–"What men are pleased to call their souls was in the hog and dog begun."

LARCOM–"I do not own an inch of land, but all I see is mine."

TROBRIDGE–"We are two travelers, Roger and I. Roger's my dog: come here, you scamp!"

CONKLIN (nominating Grant)–"He will hew to the line of right, let the chips fall where they may."

SCHURC–"Our country right or wrong. When right, to be kept right; when wrong, to be put right."

SPENCER–"With a higher moral nature will come a restriction on the multiplication of the inferior."

DICKINSON–"Glory is that right tragic thing, that for an instant means dominion, warms some poor name that never felt the sun, gently replacing in oblivion."

BROWNE–"I have already given two cousins to the war. . . I'll shed ev'ry drop of blud my able-bodied relations has got."

AUSTIN–"Gods for themselves are monuments enough."

GARNETT–"Have patience with the jealousies and petulances of actors, for their hour is their eternity."

SWINBURNE–"At the door of life, by the gate of breath, there are worst things waiting for men than death."

SYMONDS–"These things shall be, A loftier race than e'er the world hath known shall rise with flame of freedom in the souls and light of knowledge in their eyes."

WATTERSON–"Things have come to a heluva pass when a man can't cudger his own jackass."

OSLER–"Have given you the proper sense to enable you to appreciate the inconceivable droll situations in which we catch our fellow creatures."

STEVENSON–"Bright is the ring of words when the right man rings them."

SHAW–"I like a bit of a mongrel myself, whether it's a man or a dog; they're the best for every day."

ELLIS–"The place where optimism most flourishes is the lunatic asylum."

NEWBOLT–"Watch beside thine arms to-night, pray that God defends the right."

KIPLING–"Who are neither children of God, but men in a world of men."

KIPLING–"Yours is the earth and everything that's in it, and—which is more—you'll be a man, my son!"

KIPLING–"When the spirit is gone, you will discover how much you care, and will give your heart to a dog to tear."

KIPLING–"If she flatters the animal's vanity, he ends by adoring her."

FISHER–"Purity of race does not exist. Europe is a continent of energetic mongrels."

DALTON–"They, the sirens, sang the vileness of all who live contented upon an alms, and are at ease in bonds, the slaves whose servitude is made sweet by habit."

DUBOIS–"Who is good? Not that men are ignorant. What is Truth? Nay, but that men know so little of men."

KNICKERBOCKER–"I believe that when you say one is a 'Dead Game Sport' you have reached the climax of human philosophy."

KENNEDY–"The meek, the terrible meek, the fierce agonizing meek, are about to enter into their inheritance."

BAKER–"My creed may have no lift of hope for you, and yours might drive me down the slopes of hell."

MONRO–"And reaches by devious means (half smelt, half heard) the four-legged brain of a walk-ecstatic dog."

SCHAUFFLER–"At the gate of the west I stand, on the isle where the nations throng, we call them 'Scum O' the Earth'."

LETTS–"To serve us seems their only aim, asking our wishes, quick to crave our pardon, and yet I know in each of these shop people there dwells a soul withdrawn from us, elusive, the shop can never know—a secret garden."

BAILEY–"Evil and good are God's right and left hands."

RYAN–"The suffering of right are graven deepest on the chronicle of nations."

MILTON–"But made hereby obnoxious more. To all the miseries of life, life in captivity among inhuman foes."

SERVICE–"The devil enters the prompter's box and the play is ready to start."

MILTON–"Or what (though rare) of later age, ennobled hath the buckskined stage."

My being a Left gives me a unique view of things. I think that I am a very rare person, and a very old Left. My mind is very much like the Phoenix. It has been burned to ashes and is rising up stronger than ever. My God has told me to, "Fear none of those things which thou shalt suffer." With God with me, who can be against me?

THE SON-SUN

"The one great God looked down and smiled, and counted each his loving child; for Turk and Brahmin, Monk and Jew, had reached him through the Gods they knew."

—HARRY ROMAINE

The only way words make sense to me is how I interpret them. In most English literature, including the Bible, there is a double meaning. There is a literal meaning and a spiritual meaning, and in some cases there is a third meaning, which may be termed metaphysical.

The universal truth that many poets write about is a world with the absence of men. This is also the perfect world. Browning says that what he calls God, fools call nature. Thoreau maintained that rather than love, money, or fame, he would have truth.

God is light. The sun is light. What is the relationship between God and the sun? Could it be a very old mathematical theorem? There is an old saying that all energy comes from God. This statement can easily be believed if God is the sun.

The Rights are very tight-lipped about giving any correct information about this to Lefts. As I gain understanding about the parameters of the spiritual world, God is giving me closure.

Poets often write about "Fire in the Chest." This fire could be called the heart, soul, or spirit.

KIPLING–"Many religious people are deeply suspicious. They seem—for purely religious purposes, of course—to know more about iniquity than the unregenerate."

The following are some ideas about the son, sun:

GARRICK–"Let others hail the rising sun: I bow to that whose course is run."

WASHINGTON–"Labor to keep alive in your breast, that little spark of celestial fire, conscience."

WORDSWORTH–"Come forth into the light of things, let nature be your teacher."

WORDSWORTH–"The sunshine is a glorious birth; but yet I know, where'er I go, that there hath passed away a glory from the earth."

MOORE–"As half in shade and half in sun this world along its path advances, may that side the sun's upon be all that e'er shall meet thy glances!"

MOORE–"Like the stained web that whitens in the sun, grow pure by being shone upon."

BYRON–"Eternal summer gilds them yet but all, except their sun, is set."

KNOX–"The fool hath said: There is no God! No God! Who lights the morning sun, and sends him on his heavenly road, a far and brilliant course to run?"

SHELLEY–"But whose transmitted effluence can not die, so long as fire outlines the parent spark, rose, robed in dazzling immortality."

CARLYLE–"Fire is the best of servants; but what a master."

WHITTIER–"The windows of my soul I throw wide open to the sun."

ALDRICH–"But when the sun in all his state illuminated the eastern skies, she passed through glory's morning gate, and walked in paradise."

BROWNING–"Sun-threader, life and light be thine forever."

BROWNING–"God is seen God. In the star, in the stone, in the flesh, in the soul and the clod."

BROWNING–"Must in death your daylight finish? My sun sets to rise again."

BROWNING–"Sky—what a scowl of cloud till, near and far, ray on ray split the shroud: splendid, a star!"

BEECHER–"If there were no religion if that vast sphere, out of which glow all the supereminent truths of the Bible . . ."

PEARSE–"O light divine! We need no fuller test, that all is ordered well; we know enough to trust that all is best, where love and wisdom dwell."

DWIGHT–"They that work not, can not pray, can not feel the sun."

COOK–"There's a star in the west that shall never go down. Till the records of valor decay; we must worship its light."

BAILEY–"Though it's not our own, for liberty burst in its ray."

BAILEY–"The world must have great minds, even as great spheres or suns, to govern lesser restless minds."

MELVILLE–"The starred and stately nights seem haughty dames in jeweled velvets, nursing at home in lonely pride the memory of their absent conquering earls, the golden helmeted suns!"

WHITMAN–"Give me the splendid silent sun, with all his beams full-dazzling."

WHITMAN–"Not till the sun excludes you do I exclude you."

MEREDITH–"We are one with heaven and the stars when it is spent to serve God's aim: Else die we with the sun."

SWINBURNE–"To grow straight in the strength of thy spirit, and to live out thy life as the light."

DODGE–"But I believe that God is overhead; and as life is to the living, so death is to the dead."

MORLEY–"Where it is a duty to worship the sun it is pretty sure to be a crime to examine the laws of heat."

PROCTOR–"Shall bear a stalk of the tasseled corn—the sun's supreme bequest."

HARDY–"Ere systemed suns were globed and lit the slaughters of the race where writ."

BRIDGES–"Love, from the world begun, hath the secret of the sun."

COOLBRITH—"He walks with God upon the hills! And sees, each morn, the world arise new-bathed in light of paradise."

ELMSLIE—"That picture fair—the world's great light—that gazing up—the lamp between—the hand that held it scarce was seen."

SANDBURG—"For the gladness here [the Bible] where the sun is shining at evening, on the weeds of the river, our prayer of thanks."

E PLURIBUS UNUM
(ONE AMONG MANY)

Tennyson has this to say about relations between man, men: "He that wrongs his friend wrongs himself more, and ever bears about a silent court of justice in his breast, himself the judge and jury, and himself the prisoner at the bar, ever condemned."

I might add that we are betrayed by what is false within. What if a person has no spiritual brothers? Does this count for him also? The feelings of guilt and shame are certainly prevalent among Lefts. I believe that the Rights induce these feelings among Lefts. The process by which this occurs is not exactly clear to me, but I know that it occurs.

I have worked faithfully to gather knowledge concerning the term "E Pluribus Unum." The following are bits of information obtained from a wide variety of sources concerning this topic:

POPE—"Speed the soft intercourse from soul to soul, and waft a sigh from Indus to the Pole."

POPE—"Two friends, two bodies with one soul inspir'd."

BYRON—"Among them, but not of them; in a shroud of thoughts which were not their thoughts."

CARLYLE—"The lightning—spark of thought, generated or say rather heaven—kindled, in the solitary mind, awakens its express likeness in another mind, in a thousand other minds, and all blaze up together in combined fire."

GARRISON—"My country is the world; my countrymen are mankind."

LYTTON—"Every man has his price, I will bribe left and right."

HAMMOND (speech before U.S. Senate, 1858)—"The very mudsills of society . . . We call them slaves . . . But I will not characterize that class at the north with that term; but you have it. It is there, it is everywhere; it is eternal."

LONGFELLOW—"But in quiet self-control link together soul and soul."

HOLMES–"One flag, one land, one heart, one hand, one nation, evermore!"

FIELDS–"It transmutes aliens into trusting friends, and gives its owner passport round the world."

BARRY–"But whether on the scaffold high or in the battle's van, the fittest place where man can die is where he dies for man!"

LOWELL–"The story of one man's real experience finds its startling parallel in that of every one of us."

WHITMAN–"In the faces of men and women I see God."

CURTIS–"His heart in his hand, like a palm branch, waving all discords into peace, helps our faith in God, in ourselves, and in each other, more than many sermons."

CRALK–"Two to the world for the world's work safe, but each unto each, as in thy sight, one."

DICKINSON–"I'm nobody! Who are you? Are you nobody too?"

ROSSETTI–"In life our absent friend is far away: But death may bring our friend exceeding near."

SWINBURNE–"The word of the earth in the ears of the world, was it God? Was it man?"

ADAMS–"Friends are born, not made."

BUTTERWORTH–"One taper lights a thousand . . . and the humblest light may kindle a brighter than its own."

KIPLING–"For the Colonel's Lady an' Judy O'Grady are sisters under their skin."

OXENHAM–"Kneel always when you light a fire."

JOHNSON–"I have not spoken of these things, save to one man, and unto God."

RATHOM– "The 'unknown' dead? Not so: We know him well. . . . He is all brothers dead, all lovers lost, all sons and comrades resting there."

MOODY– "Shall all the happy shipmates then stand singing brotherly?"

BARY– "Why should you sing aloft, apart? Sing to the heaven of my heart; In me, In me, In me is God."

ANDERSON– "Every*one* in the world is Christ and they are crucified." [Author's italics.]

CLARK– "Let us no more be true to boasted race or clan, but to our highest dream, the brotherhood of man."

BAKER– "I love the friendly faces of old sorrows; I have no secrets that they do not know."

LINDSAY– "To live in mankind is far more than to live in a name, to live in mankind, far, far more . . . Than to live in a name."

IMMORTALITY

The most frightful idea that has ever corroded human nature is the idea of eternal punishment—the present being only a piece of eternity. Is time a linear function?

PLATO wrote–"Know Thyself." I will go one further–"Know thy Spirit." Death is the ugly fact which nature has to hide, and she does it well.

While setting down these thoughts there must be no compromise. There must also be no pleasure on my part except the fact of pleasing God. That in itself is enough. As I have stated, I believe that I have spiritual brothers somewhere in this world. If I met a spiritual brother it would be as two ships passing in the night.

The devil is very busy. He has very little time for me. The Rights, however, keep me fairly on my toes. Is everyone against me? I have become an expert at picking up vibes. This gift could have Biblical implications: discernment of the spirits. Many times I speak in metaphors and dichotomies. This comes with no effort of my own. Sometimes I reflect on what I have said and observe the reactions of the people around me. It's quite a sight!

So! Is every*one* around me against me? Yes! Is every*body* around me against me? No! When Satan turns it up a notch, God turns it up a notch. One on God's side is a majority.

The following are some famous quotes on the idea of immortality.

POPE– "Hope springs eternal in the human breast; man never is but always to be, blest." And, "All are but parts of one stupendous whole, whose body nature is, and God the soul."

WORDSWORTH– "Though inland far we be, our souls have sight of that immortal sea which brought us hither."

CLAY– "To live in hearts we leave behind is not to die."

MORE– "This narrow isthmus 'twixt two boundless seas, the past, the future, two eternities."

DANA– "A voice within us speaks the startling word, man, thou shalt never die."

KEATS– "Bards of passion and of mirth, ye have left your souls on earth! Have ye souls in heaven too?"

And, "Four seasons fill the measure of the year; there are four seasons in the mind of man."

MACAULAY– "Out of his surname they have coined an epithet for a knave, and out of his Christian name a synonym for the devil."

EMERSON– "And striving to be man the worm mounts through all the spires of form."

EMERSON– "The world uncertain comes and goes, the lover stays rooted." And, "All mankind loves a lover." Also, "Shallow men believe in luck."

CHIVERS– "To the genius of eternity crying, come to me! Come to me!"

LONGFELLOW– "Dust thou art, to dust returnest was not spoken of the soul." And, "There is no death! What seems so is transitions." Also, "The grave itself is but a covered bridge leading from light to light, through a brief darkness."

WHITTIER– "Death seems a covered way which opens into light."

BONAR–"The star is not extinguished when it sets upon the dull horizon; it but goes to shine in other skies, then reappear in ours, as fresh as when it first arose."

CHASE–"The constitution, in all its provisions, looks to an indestructible union composed of indestructible states."

A. JOHNSON–"We are swinging round the circle."

GLADSTONE–"From morn to eventide in quick, successive train, an infant lived and died and lived again."

PARKER–"All men desire to be immortal."

BROWNING–"All service ranks the same with God: With God whose puppets, best and worst, are we; there is no last nor first."

MANNERS–"Names that shall live for yet unnumbered years."

CROSS–"O may I join the choir invisible, of those immortal dead who live again in minds made better by their presence."

HOWE–"I gave my son a palace and a kingdom to control: the palace of his body, the kingdom of his soul."

LOWELL–"Great truths are the portions of the soul of man: Great souls are portions of eternity."

And, "All thoughts that mould the age begin deep within the primitive soul."

MELVILLE–"Sailor or landsman, there is some sort of Cape Horn for all. Boys! Beware of it; prepare for it in time. Gray beards! Thank God it is passed."

WENTWORTH–"Age, I make light of it, fear not the sight of it, time's but our playmate, whose toys are divine."

BUNGAY–"No Hell! Rang out the universalist bell."

MEREDITH–"Look on her grave and see not death but life."

ROSSETTI–"Beyond the sea of death love lies. For ever, yesterday, to-day."

SMITH–"The man who in this world can keep the whiteness of his soul, is not likely to lose it in any other."

HARDY–"Fear of death has even bygone us: Death gave us all that we possess."

JACKSON–"Oh, write of me not, 'Died in bitter pains' But 'Emigrated to another star'!"

INGERSOLL–"Is there beyond the silent night an endless day? Is death a door that leads to light? We cannot say."

LOCKE–"The contract 'twixt Hannah, God and me, was not for one or twenty years, but for eternity."

THOMSON–"Dateless oblivion and divine repose."

THAXTER–"Sad soul, take comfort, nor forget that sunrise never failed us yet."

WINTER–"And, lucid in that second birth I shall discern, what all the sages of the earth have died to learn."

HOWELLS–"And before you know me gone eternity and I are one."

MORLEY–"Every man of us has all the centuries in him."

SYMONDS–"No seed shall perish which the soul has sown."

BUCHANAN–"I saw the starry tree eternity put forth the blossom time."

CONRAD–"Why should a man certain of immortality think of his life at all?"

HALL–"Will last while ages roll, for that beautiful unseen temple was a child's immortal soul."

WHITE–"But the soul of her, the glowing, gorgeous, fervent soul of her, surely was flaming in eager joy upon some other dawn."

ROBINSON–"Death, like a friend unseen, shall say to me, 'My toil is over and my work begun.'"

TWEEDSMUIR–"Shall pass from strength to strength and scale the steeps of immortality."

THAYER–"Here is a toast that I want to give to a fellow I'll never know; to the fellow who's going to take my place when it's time for me to go."

PART 4

An Odyssey

When I first became ill I was paranoid and in great tribulation. I was at my father's house. Most people in my situation would choose the ultimate refuge—death. Cars were going around my father's house. I went to bed in the dark. A spirit hit me, then another hit me. I got up and went to my father and told him that God had something special for me to do. That special thing is to find the truth! All of it.

My father, a born-again Christian, told me once how he was "saved." He said that he was praying and he looked up and saw a cross with the sun superimposed on it. That does not tell me much, except that the sun is very important. As I continue my odyssey, I reflect on the words of others.

KEYSER–"The sovereign impulse of man is to find the answer to this question: What abides?"

ANONYMOUS–"But true love is a lasting fire, which viewless vestals tend, that burns forever in the soul and knows not change, nor end."

PLATO (The Apology for Socrates)–"But now it is time for us to go. I go to death, and you to life; and which of us goes to the better state is known to none but God."

SHELLEY–"Man, one harmonious soul of many a soul, whose nature is its own divine control. Gentleness, virtue, wisdom, and endurance; these are the spells by which to resume; an empire o'er the disentangled doom."

JONES–"Then no more lamented he the wingless minds of men."

BLAKE–"God appears, and God is light, to those poor souls who dwell in night; but does a human form display, to those who dwell in realms of day."

TENNYSON–"On God and godlike man we build our trust."

MEREDITH–"His art can take the eyes from out my head, until I see with eyes of other men."

BROWNING–"Life, how and what is it? As here I lie in this state-chamber, dying by degrees."

BLUNT–"Till in his turn the Turk had learned to wear the purple and fine linen of the state."

FRENCH–"What form of glory or shadow-form, fate, state of king, priest, harlot, hunted criminal?"

BROWNING–"O thou soul of my soul! I shall clasp thee again, and with God be the rest."

ROSSETTI–"Better by far you should forget and smile than that you should remember and be sad."

SHELLEY–"Through death and birth, to a diviner day."

KEATS–"And seal the hushed casket of my soul."

WHITMAN–"I shall look for loving crops from the birth, life, death, immortality, I plant so lovingly now."

RUSSEL–"Time does not affect the immortal soul." And, "Oh light our life in Babylon, but Babylon has taken wings, while we are the calm and proud procession of eternal things." Also, "Where was thy place, O light of lights? The flame of beauty far in space—where rose the fire; in thee? In me? Which bowed the elemental race to adoration silently?" Then, "In the fire of love we live, or pass by many ways, by the unnumbered ways of dream, to death."

ELIOT ("The Hollow Men")–"This is the way the world ends: Not with a bang but a whimper."

ANONYMOUS–"The mark of man, his mingled pleasure and pain, and all that the world has suffered, comes of the strife between the will of the soul and the will of life, and the clash of these in the brain."

JOHNSON–"The purpose of literature is to help man to enjoy life, or to endure it."

VAUGHAN–"I saw eternity the other night, like a great ring of pure and endless light. . . This ring the bridegroom did for none provide, but for his bride."

MILTON–"The mind is its own place and in itself can make a heaven of hell, a hell of heaven." And, "For who can think submission? War, then, war open or understood must be resolved."

DANTE–"Every country as Dante has well observed, exists everywhere in parts and nowhere as a whole."

HARDY ("Woman About to be Hanged")–"Why, since it made you sound in the germ, It sent a worm."

At one time I thought everybody was under the same moral code. Then I thought that the Rights have one set of codes, and the Lefts had another set of codes. Now I have come to realize that everybody has his own set of moral codes, custom made. Death is also custom made.

There is a line of thought which states that morals are nothing but vehicles used by Rights to control Lefts. The emotions of men have changed not one whit from the time of Aristotle. Many very intelligent people believe that human emotions are nothing but excess baggage.

Here are some examples of emotion-creating situations I have experienced:

When in college, a group of us piled into a car and headed to South Carolina to drink beer. Speeding, we came around a curve fast and hit, head on, an old hound dog in the middle of the road. Everyone laughed. One student said, "He is gone to that big boneyard in the sky."

Then down at Arnold's one day a farmer caught an opossum in a rabbit box. One man hooked the animal in the mouth and pulled him out of the box with a pair of pliers. The other man beat him to death with a hammer.

Another time a man shot a deer with an arrow and only wounded it. He told me that the deer ran through the woods and he could hear the arrow clacking on the trees.

Last summer a "friend" of mine and I planted about a dozen tomato plants at his home. One day when I went over to see the plants, he was sitting in the front yard. He told me to go around back. I saw that someone had poured gasoline on the plants.

When I was in the U.S. Army a sergeant asked me to go fox hunting with him. After the dogs cornered the fox in his den, the sergeant cut a two-pronged branch from a bush. He sharpened the prongs and then ran them into the hole. Twisting the fur of the fox, the sergeant pulled the animal out. When the dogs jumped on the fox, I could hear bones cracking. The fox let out a desperate yell: his last yell. The sergeant said that he would not have killed the fox if it had not been for the young dogs in the pack.

These are just a few examples of Rights playing on my emotions. God gave me strength.

Another Right was a member of a hunt club. He begged me to go to the club with him. He told me that they would kill another deer if I would go with him.

One night I had been out drinking with a "friend," Karol. It was very late, and a trooper was behind me. I saw him in my mirror and said to Karol, "There is a patrolman behind me." At once he grabbed the steering wheel and turned it. I was pulled over and arrested for D.W.I. On some bad advice, I refused the breathalyzer. I lost my driver's license for six months. The logistics of my getting to work and back were horrendous. The Rights will try to put more on the Lefts than they can stand.

Just because the Rights have the spirit, they feel as though they are superior to the Lefts. The Lefts are in a type of bondage known as "chattel slavery." This leads to a situation known as code duello.

There are numerous definitions and ways to measure different types of intelligence. One definition of genius is this: a genius is a person who can find a pattern in a seeming jumble of facts.

Now about control. An old professor told me, "If you believe that something is true, it is true—at least as far as you are concerned." Only another mind can prove you wrong. That mind is not infallible.

Knowing that the Rights can monitor my thoughts gives me some power. My mother has fun telling me what she is going to fix for supper. She carefully and graphically describes each item on the menu. She becomes upset if I do not play her game.

My mother can hardly hear. She turns on the TV wide open. When I take her somewhere in my car, she complains about the radio being on. I turn on the radio very low, so low that I know she cannot hear it. She says "Oh, turn that noise off, I can't stand it." Now, I know full well that she cannot hear it.

I told her that I could not understand how she could hear the radio turned on low and could not hear the TV wide open. She told me that I would never understand. I now know why she would not allow me to play the radio. The music would interfere with her monitoring my thoughts.

When I was young and did something wrong, my mother would tell me to go get a switch. She would say that if I got a big switch, she would not hit me so many times, but if I got a little switch, she would hit me many times.

This leads me to thoughts about corporal punishment versus mental punishment. If a child is made to understand right from wrong, he will almost always do what is correct. Corporal punishment is unnecessary. However, man has tremendous power to choose between right and wrong.

At times—although infrequently—I use the power of my own thought. I can imagine a brick, or sometimes hell. I am gradually gaining power over my conscious mind—also my unconscious mind. I know that God is with me or I would not last thirty minutes.

More than occasionally I am short changed when purchasing something. This occurs just enough to make me unsure after an exchange. Whether a transaction is correct is not the point; the point is to put doubt in my mind.

I am having trouble finding other Lefts. I feel that I am very old for a Left. On several occasions I have thought I had found a Left, but I have been wrong each time. All Rights conceal the spiritual world.

My old "friend" Lunnie had pleasure telling me about what happened once when he was in DTs (delirium tremens). He said a little black man would look in the window and stick out his tongue. He said he ended up throwing a radio through the window. I wonder if the image I formed was formed from his words or if he put the image directly into my mind. I believe the latter.

My speech is gradually becoming a dichotomy, through no effort of my own. I will give you just one example. An old man, whom I liked, came up to me and said, "How are you doing?" I replied, "I'm not breaking any records." The old man started trembling and immediately left. I did not intend to upset this old man.

Lately, when I make a statement I will reflect on what I said. It is a dichotomy.

I knew that I was different from other children at an early age. My mother would dress me up like a little clown and send me to school. I wanted very much to be like my peers and be accepted by them. My mother refused to allow me to be like other kids. All of my peers picked on me, including a little girl in a full body cast with polio.

I believe some spirits can exist out of a body. I make this statement from experience. The genie in the bottle may not be so far-fetched.

The Rights cannot bear for the Lefts to have any pleasure whatsoever. If it is a drinking situation, there is not enough alcohol or the Left has to worry about driving and drinking. Once I was at a dinner party and ran out of liquor. A man that sat beside me had a whole fifth. I looked at that bottle and never wanted anything so badly in my life. This was entertainment for the Rights.

I know for a fact that when voting, Rights know how the Lefts vote. The secret ballot is a joke.

When I was in college, I knew a student who was taking swimming lessons. He urinated in the pool and the instructor called him out. The instructor had caused him to urinate.

I asked Mom this question: "Why did you ever have me in the first place?" She answered, "Because I wanted something to call my own." Could anything be so hideous as one person's possessing another person?

I asked an old man if he believed that you are paid back for your sins in this life. He quickly replied, "Damn right." I had the faith all my life that the wrongs that people did to me would balance out in the long run.

An old friend of mine told me many jokes. When we were with other people he would insist that I tell the joke. The joke was my mind's image.

There is no doubt that the Rights monitor my prayers. I don't care, because they cannot do anything about the content and sincerity.

When in jail at Greensboro, I saw a very strange vision. I cannot explain it, but I saw Hitler's ovens. I am beginning to realize that some of my most fundamental beliefs are not correct. Did the Holocaust happen as it is written in the textbook? From what I know about the Germans and Jews, it is much more likely that the Jews gassed the Germans. At any rate, the spirit was behind it all—the spirit of Satan.

Once I read *Animal Farm*, by George Orwell. It is a book about animals who have human names and human characteristics. In the end there are some sheep in a pen with an electric fence around it. After a few days the electric wire is removed and replaced by a string. How long will the string work?

Satan-worship has been in some families for many generations—a thousand years in some cases. Christians need Satan, for if there were no evil, there would be no need for Christianity. Satan is in charge of the physical world and God, the spiritual.

At a Christian meeting I sat across the table from a thirtyish, heavy-set man who said he was a judge. I picked up his vibes, and I believe he was a judge—a judge for Satan.

Something that has always been a mystery to me is the pyramid on a dollar bill with the seeing eye. The pyramid represents the lore of the ancient people. The seeing eye represents the all-seeing spirit, maybe the Holy Spirit, maybe another spirit. I have been contending with the physical world and have been ignorant of the spiritual world all my life. I have dealt with the physical world on my terms. My knowledge of the spiritual world is increasing exponentially. Almost every day God reveals something new to me.

When I was in tribulation in my schoolroom, some of the students told me that I was the devil. I told them that they were the devil. Who was the devil? My idea of the devil is a spirit that destroys people. This idea fits the students to a tee.

Here is something that I need to mention: the subliminal control of nations. The nations are primarily the Lefts. With our modern computers and electronic expertise it is easy to understand how super computers could subliminally control people, especially the Lefts.

Here is some evidence that Rights can get information from Lefts, even if it is not in the conscious mind of the Left. A wealthy businessman from Haw River was in a bar one day, and I joined him for a beer. He was a very nice man. He began talking to me about a very crafty old man from Haw River. His name was John Thompson. His daughter was a friend of my mother. I may have seen this man two or three times when I was four or five years old. How did this man know that I knew John Thompson? The plot thickens!

When I was teaching, there was a student who gave me much trouble. I confronted him about a certain situation. I wanted to beat the hell out of him, but I couldn't, and he knew it. The student planted his feet and wiggled his hips, daring me to do something. An old "friend" of mine, with the same exact morphology as the student, exhibited the same exact behavior when I would see him.

Sometimes when a thought comes to me I can do some mental backtracking and find the origin of the thought. I am getting better and better at this. It is imperative that I master this. I am dismantling my prison. Habits begin as cobwebs and end as cables. Through recent times my mind is becoming much stronger.

Through my life I have lent money to some nice people. They never paid me back, but I continued to like them. Now I know that Rights are not supposed to repay Lefts. Lefts are second class citizens in every sense of the term.

Some professors will teach their students that there are two kinds of people, the tough- and the tender-minded, and that only the tough-minded will survive. Is this true? There is such a thing as altruism. There is also such a thing as love.

As Milton wrote in *Paradise Lost*, "War whether open or understood must be resolved."

More and more I am beginning to recognize this life as a facade. The Rights are on one side and the Lefts on the other. It is almost like the game of who will blink first. Going through the physical activities of the day, I try to keep my mind on physical things.

The Rights have ninety-nine percent of the knowledge and ninety-nine percent of the wisdom. It is the one percent they lack that will do them in.

JOHNSON–"For all the great religions that the world has ever seen are contaminated with human blood: Christianity, Judaism, Islam, Hinduism, Buddhism. Each has a dreadful record of fermenting fratricidal strife. The reason, no doubt, is that in every such case the religion has been perverted from its original function. . . I know of none that cannot be, or that has not been at some time prostituted to the service of murderous passion."

BLAKE–"Since all the riches of the world may be gifts from the devil and earthly kings, I should suspect that I worshipped the devil if I thanked my God for worldly things."

PART 5

Gideon, the Sixth Judge

The Modern Gideons apparently do good work. They place Bibles in prisons, schools, hospitals, and motels. Are these Bibles meant to convert people who come in contact with them to Christianity? Gideon, the sixth judge, had in mind only to have his enemies slay themselves. The last thing he had in mind was to convert his enemies to Judaism or anything else.

"The Israelites surrounded the Midianites at night and the three hundred Israelites blew trumpets and the Lord set every man's sword against his fellow."

–Judges 7:21

In other words, he caused them to commit suicide. I must conclude that there is a wide gap between the motives of the modern Gideons and the motives of the Gideons of old . . . or is there?

Once, several years ago, I was in great tribulation in a motel room. I got the Gideon Bible and began to study it. I could not understand it. I tried everything. Nothing worked. If I had had my pistol with me, I realize now that I might have used it.

Here is what two elderly men told me. One declared, "The Bible will drive you crazy if you don't watch out." The other, a Gideon, said, "Turn it loose, and the Bible will defend itself."

In the Bible there are many references to "Lord God." This implies that there is more than one God. The term "Kingdom of God" refers to the soul of the believer, while the term "Kingdom of Heaven" refers to the souls of the believers collectively. The streets of gold are streets of liquid gold (oil, asphalt). The many mansions have been built and are being built now.

Recently I have come in contact with people with whom I had financial dealings in the past. Some of these people I liked very much. When they were in my presence, they trembled. I knew.

Why does God take some people who are apparently good, but let others, who are apparently evil, live to a ripe old age? Only God knows the heart.

One of the most difficult endeavors I have undertaken is control of my own thought processes. When I am alone it is most difficult. Everybody wants a little time to be their own person, to practice their little idiosyncrasies. This is not possible for me; I am being constantly monitored.

I have no wife and no children. An old man told me, "God don't make no mistakes." I replied, "No, but people do."

The command to fear God is in the Bible numerous times. I have heard all my life that so-and-so is a God-fearing man, meaning that he is a good man. My question is this: if God is omnipotent, why does he require men to fear him?

All through my life, I have remembered insignificant facts. I wondered through the years why I retained such facts. Now they are becoming valuable. These insignificant facts are beginning to fall into place and form closure.

I have found through experience that the biggest deceivers are those who do not lie. How about the teacher with her back to the class? She seems to have eyes in the back of her head. What she really has is the "spirit."

Here is a relevant quote from F.D.R.: "We have nothing to fear but fear itself." What kind of hokum is it that translates into one word: fear?

For a while I dated a professor at U.N.C.G. We had a most unusual relationship. She was offered a job in Maryland and she took it. She wrote a letter to me and ended each paragraph with the word sanguine. I did not understand it then, but I do now.

I am now trying to decipher the boundary between the physical and the spiritual. I have found that when I am in conversation with

Confessions of a Dandy

one or more people and I bring up a topic to discuss that is spiritual in nature, I open a floodgate. If I am careful in what I say, there are certain topics that they cannot bring up.

If I show aggressive behavior, then the Rights can show aggressive behavior. If I show fear, the Rights can take advantage of this. Fear is the Rights' most powerful weapon. However, if you are a Left and have God with you, you have nothing to fear. Here is a very good verse in the Bible that I live by:

"Wherefore let him that thinketh he standeth take heed lest he fall."

–1 Corinthians 10:12.

It is odd that both God and Satan require sacrifices. It is also odd that Jews can execute Gentiles but cannot execute Jews, no matter how awful the crime.

Let me mention a line in a very famous hymn, "The Old Rugged Cross," "At the cross where a world of lost sinners was slain." What does this line mean? Was the old man slain and replaced by the new man? Or was it something far more sinister?

Satan loves man and hates men. I do not care whether man forgives me, as long as God does.

Let me write a bit about "niggers." Niggers are people who lack complexion. They are what I call Lefts. Skin color has nothing to do with the term. There is a bar out in the county that prohibits niggers from entering. If niggers want beer, they must go to a window to be served. Once I was prevented from entering and had to go to the nigger window. I did not catch on at the time, but I do now.

When Linnaeus first developed the binomial system of nomenclature, the scientific name of man was *Homo duplex*. This means *two parts*, physical and spiritual. Later the appellation was changed to *Homo sapiens*, which means *wise man*. We were not very modest in naming ourselves. I believe the former name is more appropriate.

Here is a peculiar distinction between two races, Aryan and Mediterranean. When Aryans talk to each other, they stand about six feet apart, while the Mediterraneans stand only three feet apart. It is evolutionary. Do you understand?

Several years ago a girl and I went to the beach. We could not find a room at that beach so we drove to another beach. On the way we stopped at a rest area and used the rest room. When I entered the rest room I met Lunnie, who was with his daughter. The chance of my running into someone I knew at random was zero. Coincidence?

Another strange coincidence was my receiving my draft notice from President Kennedy. I not only received my draft notice the day that he was killed, but at the very minute of his death.

A teacher at U.N.C.G. told me, "Every thought possible to be thought has already been thought."

The many times that I have been in institutions, not one of my "friends" asked about it. They knew.

During the last several years, no fewer than five wives of men I knew made passes at me. I had a brief affair with one of them. Now I am fully aware that I am not that desirable a person. The ulterior motive must have been a setup.

My grandfather was a great fox hunter. At one time he had thirty-five Walker hounds. When I was young he would occasionally take me fox hunting. Now what these hunters enjoy is called "the race." The hunters would listen to the dogs and could tell what was happening. What most people do not perceive is the fear of the fox; the hunters relish it. One English writer describes a fox hunt thus, "The unspeakable after the uneatable."

My motive for writing this paper is not the bashing of Rights. There are many Rights whom I love. My motive is to find the truth, even if it hurts other people, even if it hurts me.

About a year after I left the work force on medical retirement, I decided to visit my school. When I arrived I went to the front office. The secretary, a very competent woman, started waving her arms like a windmill. My reception in the teachers' lounge was ice cold.

I am now realizing the extent to which the spiritual world controls the physical world.

> "The world's a theater, The earth a stage,
> Which God and nature Do with actors fill."
>
> –Shakespeare

The wise know this.

Let me mention an event that happened during a class at U.N.C.G. A professor asked the question, "Who knows what the term phlogiston means?" I knew what it meant, so I raised my hand. As soon as I raised my hand my mind went blank. This is one of many times "stumbling blocks" have been used on me.

The American Indians in upstate New York have near perfect balance. This is evolutionary. They are comfortable walking on a six-inch beam hundreds of feet above the ground. Their ancestors evolved during the Pleistocene, or Ice, Age. During this time, only the sure-footed survived.

I have long suspected that my parents were not my parents, but the evidence to prove this is quite skimpy, having only two elements: the Indian song mentioned in Paper One and the hair pattern on my chest. My father has a large amount of hair on his chest, as had my maternal grandfather. Hair pattern is hereditary. I have no hair on my chest whatsoever. Neither do Indians.

Once I was in great tribulation and walked through the woods. I began singing to the trees, as if they were Indians. When I was a little boy my mother bought an Indian tom-tom for me. She also bought me an Indian head dress and a bow and arrows. Something that I remember reading is the fact that Hitler very much admired the way that Grant handled the Indians.

Here is the story about dope. The pusher can give a prospective buyer the real thing and then switch. If the buyer is a Left, the pusher, a Right, can project a sense of pleasure in the Left. Then he sells sugar to the Left.

I have read in the past that the Mormon elders periodically meet with God in a special room in the temple. Now, I don't want to go out on a limb, but I don't know whom they meet.

Cleanliness is next to godliness, some say. The soul of a Right is just beneath the skin. You should keep your skin clean. Here are a few words from the Bible about sanctification:

"And I will be sanctified in you before the heathen," Ezekiel 20:41; "And am sanctified in them in the sight of many nations," Ezekiel 39:27 "That the offering up of the Gentiles might be acceptable being sanctified by the Holy Ghost," Romans 15:16. "For by one offering he hath perfected for ever them that are sanctified," Hebrews 10:14

A lifelong "friend" of mine, a Right, was bisexual, but mostly heterosexual. He had a magnetic personality. He was also a very heavy drinker. He would tell me about bisexual experiences that he had had. Mostly, they were very funny. Somehow it was okay for him to behave in this manner. It is not okay for me to behave in this manner. I had one bisexual experience in my life, and you would think that I had shot the Pope.

What is the difference? Is there one set of standards for the Rights and another set of standards for the Lefts? This "friend" would sometimes say, "A man told me this, a man told me that." I never asked the obvious question: who is this man?

The poor female Lefts are helpless to resist the advances of the male Rights, and the female Rights control the male Lefts almost at will. There is a song from the 1940s called "That Old Black Magic (Called Love)."

Being a Left, it has been my experience that a female Right can cause me to be aroused, or she can prevent me from becoming aroused. I, truthfully, do not understand rape.

An old man told me this: "There are two types of people, the caught and the uncaught." Another old saying goes, "If you can't dazzle them with brilliance, baffle them with bullshit."

There are some things that the Rights cannot deny. There are certain math problems that only the Rights can solve. A Right will tell a Left that only one man can solve this problem.

If I think or say the above thought and there is a Right in my presence, he answers, loud and clear, "That's Right." Also, if I bring up a spiritual subject and what I say is true, the Rights invariably say emphatically, "That's Right!"

As a retired school teacher, I understand what has been going on in public schools recently. The curriculum is gradually shifting to the benefits of the Rights. However, I believe it is a crime for the teachers not to teach *all* of the students the truths about the spiritual worlds.

Several months ago a very young waitress at the Waffle House approached me and gave me a big, sincere hug. She said to me, "You are so old." A student at my school also said that to me.

The Rights try to prejudice the Lefts against other races. They will whisper terms like nigger or Jap or Mexican, spoken in a derogatory manner. This ploy does not work on me because I have always respected other races—even more than my own race!

There is a limit to the effectiveness of fear. If a Left has taken all of the fear that the devil can dish out, the law of diminishing returns takes place. In Ephesians 6:12 are these words: "For we wrestle not against flesh and blood, but against principalities, against powers, against the rulers of the darkness of this world, against spiritual wickedness in high places."

Having written these papers, I know they are not perfect. I am very much aware that there are all sorts of errors in them. After I have finished a paper and I think that it is fairly well written, the mistakes begin to come to me. There comes a point in time, however, when I must say this paper is finished, mistakes and all.

"If this be error and upon me proved I never writ, nor no man ever loved."

–Shakespeare

Confessions of a Dandy

Poetry as Paradigm

Poetry cannot be defined, it can only be described. The sound of a poem, like its diction and imagery, can be evaluated only in relation to its total design. One must also consider the poet, for the work is framed—whether by design or natural law—on the basis of what the writer is seen to be: storyteller, singer, wit and humorist, portrayer of character, elegist, critic, or philosopher.

Much poetry is based on the life cycle of man. Sometimes the life cycle is portrayed by the time of day: morning, noon, evening and night. Sometimes the life cycle is described as the year: spring, summer, fall, and winter. In all the poems I have read concerning the life cycle of man (and there are many), I have never seen the word *reincarnation*. This is very strange, because this is what the poems are about. Is someone attempting to conceal something from somebody?

Interpreting poetry can be risky business, but that is what I propose to do, in order to illustrate the philosophy which I have tried to set forth. To do this, I have taken phrases out of context and, with a sentence or two, attempted to explain their meaning in the framework of my investigation of truth. Whether I have set myself an impossible task must be judged on the merits of what I have wrought.

"The Griesly Wife"
by John Manifold

Oh, long the fire may burn for him
And open stand the door,
And long the bed may wait empty:
He'll not be back any more.

This is the story about a man and his uncanny ("griesly") young bride. She runs out the door, barefoot, into the snow. The man follows her tracks in the snow and sees that "the two bare feet gave out and a four-foot track went on." The fire in the opening line above is hell. The four-foot creature is the earth.

"A Soldier"
by Robert Frost

See nothing worthy to have been its mark,
It is because like men we look too near,
Forgetting that as fitted to the sphere,
Our missiles always make too short an arc.
They fall, they rip the grass, they intersect
The curve of earth, and striking, break their own

They make us cringe for metal-point on stone.
But this we know, the obstacle that checked
And tripped the body, shot the spirit on
Further than target ever showed or shone.

This is a story about a soldier and his lance. The word "men" is mentioned in this poem because it is indiscriminate. That is, it includes both Rights and Lefts, although the term usually implies only Lefts. "Further than target ever showed or shone" means the next state for the spirit.

"In Hardwood Groves"
by Robert Frost

Before the leaves can mount again
To fill the trees with another shade,
They must go down past things coming up,
They must go down into the dark decayed.

> *They must be pierced by flowers and put*
> *Beneath the feet of dancing flowers.*
> *However it is in some other world*
> *I know that this is the way in ours.*

This is a description of the leaves and their cycle of growing, turning brown, and falling off the trees. Flowers come up through the leaves. The flowers are Rights and the leaves are Lefts.

"Strange Holiness"
by Robert P. Tristram Coffin

> *There was but a ruin there,*
> *A hunted creature, stripped and bare.*
> *Then he faded at one stroke,*
> *Like a dingy, melting smoke.*
> *But there his fish lay like a key*
> *To the bright lost mystery.*

The poem is an allegory about the Lefts, represented by the fox (the hunted creature), and the fish, which represents the possessions of the Lefts.

"The Donkey"
by G.K. Ghesterton

> *The tattered outlaw of the earth,*
> *Of ancient crooked will;*
> *Starve, scourge, deride me: I am dumb;*
> *I keep my secret still.*
>
> *Fools! For I also had my hour;*
> *One far, fierce hour and sweet.*
> *There was a shout about my ears,*
> *And palms before my feet.*

The donkey represents the Lefts. Palms "before my feet" refers to the donkey on Palm Sunday. Christ was sitting on a donkey, a Left.

"Death Be Not Proud"
by John Donne

One short sleepe past, wee wake eternally,
And Death shall be no more, Death thou shalt die.

This poem is about death and its effect on men and lack of effect on man.

"Traveler's Curse After Misdirection"
by Robert Graves

May they catch their feet and fall;
At each and every fall they take
May a bone within them break;
And may the bone that breaks within
Not be, for variation's sake,
Now rib, now thigh, now arm, now shin,
But always, without fail the neck.

The traveler symbolizes the Lefts. The poem tells about how the Lefts stumble and trip and fall step after step, mile after mile, stage after stage.

"Mr. Flood's Party"
by Edwin Arlington Robinson

The bird is on the wing, the poet says, . . .
There was not much that was ahead of him,
And there was nothing in the town below—
Where strangers would have shut the many doors
That many friends had opened long ago.

This poem is about the reflections of an old man whose death is not far off. He has a jug of whisky and reflects on the past and present. His party is himself alone.

"The bird is on the wing" means death is not far off. In most cases in poetry a bird or a bird's song symbolizes death.

"Ulysses"
by Alfred Lord Tennyson

Souls that have toiled, and wrought, and thought with me, . . .

Some work of noble note, may yet be done,
Not unbecoming men that strove with Gods.

Confessions of a Dandy

The "thought with me" is suspiciously like ol' E Pluribus Unum. This can also pertain to "strove with Gods." Why is "Gods" capitalized?

"Because I Could Not Stop For Death"
by Emily Dickinson

Because I could not stop for Death,
He kindly stopped for me;
The carriage held but just ourselves
And Immortality. . .

Since then, 'tis centuries, and yet
Feels shorter than the day
I first surmised the horses' heads
Were toward eternity.

This poem is about immortality and all that goes with it. "Since then, 'tis centuries, and yet feels shorter than the day."

Another part of the poem mentions a house that is "a swelling of the ground." This refers to a grave.

"I Think Continually of Those Who Were Truly Great"
by Stephen Spender

I think continually of those who were truly great.
Who, from the womb, remembered the soul's history
Through corridors of light where the hours are suns . . .

The names of those who in their lives fought for life,
Who wore at their hearts the fire's centre.
Born of the sun, they traveled a short while toward the sun
And left the vivid air signed with their honour.

Here is mentioned the "corridors of light" which have often been described by people who have had a near death experience.

"From the womb" indicates to me that, at least for some people, sanctification takes place in the womb; "Remembered the soul's history"—for Rights.

This poem, as most poems are, is about Rights. "Born of the sun" seems to say that the sun is God, even though "sun" is not capitalized.

"An Epitaph, A Child of Queen Elizabeth's Chapel"
by Ben Johnson

Years he numbered scarce thirteen
When fates turned cruel,
Yet three filled zodiacs had he been. . .

But, being so much too good for earth
Heaven vows to keep him.

Here, the child who died is a Right. "Yet three filled zodiacs had he been." The zodiacs are made up of stars. Stars and sand are used extensively by poets to symbolize the soul. This child was the product of many reincarnations—and going for more.

"Elegy for a Dead Soldier"
by Karl Shapiro

Shall we believe our eyes or legends rich
With glory and rebirth beyond the void?. . .

Is every fall, and this one like the rest.
However others calculate the cost,
To us the final aggregate is one . . .

Underneath this wooden cross there lies
A Christian killed in battle. You who read,
Remember that this stranger died in pain;
And passing here, if you can lift your eyes
Upon a peace kept by a human creed,
Know that one soldier has not died in vain.

Here again we read quite a bit about reincarnation. The death of one Right or many Rights is the same. "The final aggregate is one."

"Know that one soldier has not died in vain." This phrase signifies the death of a Right. He has not died in vain because his spirit lives on.

At one time I thought that the phrase was used to symbolize a soldier's death in pursuit of a worthwhile goal. I was wrong.

"In Memory of W.B. Yeats"
by W. H. Auden

But for him it was his last afternoon as himself, . . .

The words of a dead man
Are modified in the guts of the living. . .

Earth, receive an honored guest;
William Yeats is laid to rest:
Let the Irish vessel lie
Emptied of its poetry.

Time that is intolerant
Of the brave and innocent,
And indifferent in a week
To a beautiful physique.

Here the soul of W.B. Yeats goes into "a beautiful physique." Since the soul is neuter, the beautiful physique could be male or female.

"Hope"
by Randall Jarrell

The Spirit Killeth but the Letter Giveth Life. . .
Woe's me! Woe's me! In Folly's mailbox
Still laughs the postcard, Hope:
Your uncle in Australia
Has died and you are Pope.
For many a soul has entertained
A Mailman unawares—
And as you cry, "Impossible,"
A step is on the stairs.

This poem is a bit cryptic, but if your spiritual uncle died and you received his soul, his spirit could be shared with the pope. The letter is spiritual.

"Science"
by Robinson Jeffers

Man, introverted man, having crossed
In passage and but a little with the nature of things this latter
 century.
Has begot giants; but being taken up
Like a maniac with self-love and inward conflicts cannot
manage his hybrids.
Being used to deal with edgeless dreams,
Now he's bred knives on nature turns them also inward: they
have thirsty points though.
His mind forebodes his own destruction;
Actaeon who saw the goddess naked among leaves and his
hounds tore him.
A little knowledge, a pebble from the shingle,
A drop from the oceans: who would have dreamed this
infinitely little too much?

The term science is used to identify the modes of the spiritual
world. "In passage" means death and rebirth. The term "his
hybrids" refers to mules, or Lefts. I do not know whether this man
represents Lefts or Rights. The poem sends mixed signals: "A little
knowledge" . . . "a drop from the oceans" . . . is a dangerous thing.

"Terence, This Is Stupid Stuff"
by A. E. Housman

It should do good to heart and head
When your soul is in my soul's stead;
And I will friend you, if I may,
In the dark and cloudy day. . .

They poured strychnine in his cup
And shook to see him drink it up:
They shook, they stared as white's their shirt:
Them it was their poison hurt.
—I tell the tale that I heard told.
Mithridates, he died old.

Here is an example of "one among many," or soul swapping, if
you please. This part of the poem is about the king's being
poisoned with arsenic and strychnine. He lived. This illustrates that
nobody can be killed unless God wills it.

"Tempt Me No More"
by C. Day Lewis

Oh keep the sickle sharp
And follow still the plow:
Others may reap, though some
See not the winter through.

Father who endest all,
Pity our broken sleep;
For we lie down with tears
And waken but to weep.

And if our blood alone
Will melt this iron earth,
Take it. It is well spent
Easing a savior's birth.

"Others may reap, though some see not the winter through" refers to a Right-Left situation. The lines "For we lie down with tears and waken but to weep" and "Pity our broken sleep" refer to death and rebirth.

"Fern Hill"
by Dylan Thomas

In the sun born over and over . . .
And wake to the farm forever fled from the childless land.
Oh as I was young and easy in the mercy of his means,
Time held me green and dying
Though I sang in my chains like the sea.

This poem is about nature worship. "The sun born over and over" could be the son born over and over. "Childless land" describes the lot of the Lefts. The sea can describe mortality or immortality.

"In My Craft or Sullen Art"
by Dylan Thomas

Not for the towering dead
With their nightingales and psalms
But for the lovers, their arms

Round the griefs of the ages,
Who pay no praise or wages
Nor heed my craft or art.

This poem begins with a few lines about the dead (Lefts). The last few lines explain themselves. The lovers need not heed.

"Say Not the Struggle Nought Availeth"
by Arthur Hugh Clough

If hopes were dupes, fears may be liars;
It may be, in yon smoke concealed.
Your comrades chase e'en now the fliers,
And, but for you, possess the field. . .

In front, the sun climbs slow, how slowly,
But westward, look, the land is bright.

Here is a Right allied with Lefts who "But for you, possess the field."

"But westward, look, the land is bright" means that far off, death is bright for the Rights.

"Sand Dunes"
by Robert Frost

Men left her a ship to sink:
They can leave her a hut as well;
And be but more free to think
For the one more cast off shell.

The ship and hut are human bodies, as is the "cast off shell."

"I Could Give All to Time"
by Robert Frost

I could give all to Time except—except
What I myself have held. But why declare
The things forbidden that while the Customs slept
I have crossed to Safety with? For I am There,
And what I would not part with I have kept.

He held on to his soul. The customs represent the physical world.

"Karma"
by Edwin Arlington Robinson

Confessions of a Dandy

Acknowledging an improvident surprise,
He magnified a fancy that he wished
The friend whom he had wrecked were here again.
Not sure of that, he found a compromise;
And from the fullness of his heart he fished
A dime for Jesus who had died for men.

Karma is the Hindu principle by which the behavior in this life carries over into the next life. He sees a freezing Santa Claus "with his beard and bell."

"Poem"
by William Carlos Williams

carefully
then the hind
stepped down
into the pit of
the empty
flower pot

This poem is about a cat (sometimes a symbol of the devil) walking over the jam closet. The hind means a deer or simply behind the pit is hell.

"The Term"
by William Carlos Williams

The ground. Unlike
a man it rose
again rolling

with the wind over
and over to be as
it was before.

This poem is about a car crushing a brown piece of paper about the size of a man. *Unlike* a man, it returned "as it was before." In reincarnation man does not inhabit the same body.

"Success Is Counted Sweetest"
by Emily Dickinson

As he, defeated—dying—
On whose forbidden ear

The distant strains of triumph
Burst agonized and clear!

The "forbidden ear" is the ear of the Lefts. It cannot hear spiritual things.

"Split the Lark and You'll Find the Music"
by Emily Dickinson

Loose the flood, you shall find it patent,
Gush after gush, reserved for you;
Scarlet experiment! Sceptic Thomas,
Now, do you doubt that your bird was true?

This is a rather wicked poem about suicide. "Loose the flood" means blood. "Gush after gush," more blood. "Scarlet experiment," more blood.

Sceptic Thomas refers to doubting Thomas in the Bible. Sceptic means filthy. The bird or the song of a bird is used extensively as a harbinger of death.

"Nature"
by Henry Wadsworth Longfellow

So Nature deals with us, and takes away
Our playthings one by one, and by the hand
Leads us to rest so gently that we go
Scarce knowing if we wish to go or stay,
Being too full of sleep to understand
How far the unknown transcends the what we know.

This is a beautiful poem . . . for Rights. There is a good word to describe this poem: transition. Some magazines also use this term for the death of Rights. There are still some unknown aspects about the death of Rights.

"Hap"
by Thomas Hardy

But not so. How arrives it joy lies slain,
And why unblooms the best hope ever sown?

—Crass Casualty obstructs the sun and rain,
And dicing Time for gladness casts a moan . . .
These purblind Doomsters had as readily strown
Blisses about my pilgrimage as pain.

In this poem, the doomsters look at the evil side of the poet's "pilgrimage." But they do not know what they are talking about. Good wins. It is a dichotomy.

"The Man He Killed"
by Thomas Hardy

Yes; quaint and curious war is!
You shoot a fellow down
You'd treat if met where any bar is,
Or help to half-a-crown.

Two men were face to face on opposites sides in a battle. One killed the other. Under different circumstances the shooter would have bought the fallen man a drink.

"Juggler"
by Richard Wilbur

Grazing his finger ends,
Cling to their courses there,
Swinging a small heaven about his ears.

Jugglers can only be Rights. Lefts do not have the sense of body position that Rights have.

"Epistemology"
by Richard Wilbur

Kick at the rock, Sam Johnson, break your bones:
But cloudy, cloudy is the stuff of stones.

We milk the cow of the world, and as we do
We whisper in her ear, "You are not true."

"Cloudy, Cloudy" means darkened by gloom or anxiety. The cow of the world is the Lefts.

"Silence"
by Marianne Moore

My father used to say,

"Superior people never make long visits,
have to be shown Longfellow's grave
or the glass flowers at Harvard.
Self-reliant like the cat—

Superior people do not need anybody to lean on. They are self-reliant like the cat; they are Rights.

"Senex"
by John Betjeman

Oh whip the dogs away, my Lord,
They make me ill with lust.
Bend bare knees down to pray, my Lord,
Teach sulky lips to say, my Lord,
That flaxen hair is dust.

This poem is about a young male Right who is having difficulty dealing with the flesh. He prays to the Lord for help to distinguish between the physical world and the spiritual world. The "flaxen hair" represents mortality. The dogs are beautiful female Lefts.

"Sonnet to Gath"
by Edna St. Vincent Millay
Till out of loneliness, being flawed with clay,

"Being flawed with clay" represents her physical body. The mortal body is flawed.

"The Rhodora: On Being Asked, Whence is the Flower"
by Ralph Waldo Emerson

Then Beauty is its own excuse for being:
Why thou wert there, O rival of the rose!
I never thought to ask, I never knew;
But, in my simple ignorance, suppose
The self-same Power that brought me there brought you.

This very moving poem is about the worship of God through nature.

"Animula"
by T. S. Eliot

Issues from the hand of God, the simple soul . . .
Denying the importunity of the blood,

Shadow of its own shadows, spectre in its own gloom,
Leaving disordered papers in a dusty room;
Living first in the silence after the viaticum...

Pray for us now and at the hour of our birth.

Here we have the dying of an animal Left. The true Right is as concerned about his birth as he is his death.

"The Waking"
by Theodore Roethke

I wake to sleep, and take my waking slow.
I feel my fate in what I cannot fear.
I learn by going where I have to go.

This poem is about reincarnation. "Take my waking slow" means that he will stretch out the time between birth and death.

"Four Preludes on Playthings of the Wind"
by Carl Sandburg

The past is a bucket of ashes

The feet of the rats
scribble on the doorsills;
the hieroglyphs of the rat footprints
chatter the pedigrees of the rats
and babble of the blood
and gabble of the breed
of the grandfathers and the great-grandfathers of the rats.

And the wind shifts
and the dust on a doorsill shifts
and even the writing of the rat footprints
tells us nothing, nothing at all
about the greatest city, the greatest nation
where the strong men listened
and the women warbled: Nothing like us ever was.

This poem reminds me of Shelley's poem "Ozymandias," in which this line appears: "Of that colossal wreck, boundless and bare, the lone and level sands stretch far away." Both Shelley's and Sandburg's poems are about the temporal side of the physical world: Lefts.

"God's Grandeur"
by Gerard Manley Hopkins

Why do men then now not reck his rod?
Generations have trod, have trod, have trod;
And all is seared with trade; bleared, smeared with toil
And wears man's smudge and shares man's smell: the soil
Is bare now, nor can foot feel, being shod.

Here is a distinction between man and men. "Nor can foot feel being shod." Here men are working and have no idea of what they are working for: "donkey."

"Not reck his rod" means that men do not fear God. In fact they have a very murky conception of God.

"The Habit of Perfection"
by Gerard Manley Hopkins

Nostrils, your careless breath that spend
Upon the stir and keep of pride,
What relish shall the censers send
Along the sanctuary side!

O feel-of-primrose hands, O feet
That want the yield of plushy sward,
But you shall walk the golden street
And you unhouse and house the Lord.

And, Poverty, be thou the bride
And now the marriage feast begun,
And lily-coloured clothes provide
Your spouse not laboured at nor spun.

This is a very clever poem about reincarnation. "What relish . . ." means that you are taking nothing with you except the soul.

"Spring and Fall: To a Young Child"
by Gerard Manley Hopkins

Now no matter, child, the name:
Sorrow's springs are the same.

Nor mouth had, no nor mind, expressed
What heart heard of, ghost guessed
It is the blight man was born for,
It is Margaret you mourn for.

Here is a rather solemn poem about a young female Left. Knowing this explains the poem.

"The Garden of Love"
by William Blake

So I turned to the Garden of Love,
That so many sweet flowers bore:

And I saw it was filled with graves,
And tombstones where flowers should be;
And priests in black gowns were walking their rounds,
And binding with briars my joys and desires.

The flowers represent the Rights; the tombstones and briars are the Lefts.

PAPER FOUR

Searching For Truth in the Bible

PART 1
The Old Testament

My primary source here is the *Scofield Reference Version of the King James Bible*. The Old Testament was translated from Hebrew into Greek in Alexandria, Egypt, before the birth of Christ. It took seventy scholars seven years to complete this work; hence the name Septuagint.

The first five books are called the Pentateuch, and it is generally accepted that Moses was the author. In order to remain somewhat objective, I believe I must include this statement taken from the introduction to the King James Version (KJV):

"The saying that 'anything may be proved by the Bible' is both true and false—true if isolated passages are used. Utterly false if the whole divine Revelation is in view."

While I acknowledge the validity of that statement, I believe certain facts can be gleaned from specific passages. Ignoring the Bible in my search for truth would be a greater error than I risk in isolating only certain parts. It is the only way I can proceed.

GENESIS

Genesis 1:1

"In the beginning God created the heavens and the earth."

This is the Holy grail of physics: changing energy into matter.

Genesis 1:3

"And God said, let there be light: and there was light."

There are two cases of the sun going dark, excluding solar eclipses, to my knowledge: my personal experience on Highway 54 and the occurrence in Philadelphia during the first Continental Congress, during which the sun went dark and stayed dark for more than three hours. Who can turn the sun off and on? God? Satan? Both?

Here is one definition of *day* out of the footnotes of a Bible: "A period of time, long or short, during which certain revealed purposes of God are to be accomplished." Attempting to be somewhat objective, I do not think I have the latitude to accept that definition of *day*.

God created the heavens and the earth, the firmament (heaven), land and sea, plant life, sun, moon, stars, animal life, man.

Genesis 1:8

"And God called the firmament heaven. And the evening and the morning were the second day."

Webster defines heaven as the vault or arch of the sky. According to this definition, heaven could extend millions of light years into space (among the stars), or one inch above the earth.

Genesis 1:27

"So God created man in his own image, in the image of God created He him; male and female created He them."

Blake acknowledged "the brotherhood of Eden" [mankind]. The KJV footnotes also state that "man was created, not evolved." Yet the fossil record and contemporary observation are direct and powerful evidence in support of organic evolution. Some indirect evidences are: embryology, comparative anatomy, and the fact that the basis of life is similar. Organic evolution is accepted today as fact by all serious students of biology. It is this spirit business that arouses my interest.

It is of little doubt that the human body is the result of human genetics, but the spirit is another matter. To the delight of Buck

Rogers fans, the spirit could have come to earth in the last few millennia. The human body would be already developed and ready for the spirit to take up residence inside.

Genesis 2:8

"And the Lord God planted a garden eastward in Eden; and there He put the man whom He had formed."

This is the first covenant: the Edenic. There are seven more covenants in the Bible. A covenant is a solemn agreement. To make it short: Adam and Eve disobeyed God and were expelled from the garden. Hence we come to the second, or Adamic, covenant. This covenant gives conditions of life to fallen man; hard, in return for his disobedience.

CAIN AND ABEL

Cain, the farmer, slew Abel, the shepherd, because Cain's offering was not accepted by God; murder.

Genesis 4:14

Here Cain speaks to God: *"Behold, thou hast driven me out this day from the face of the earth; and from thy face shall I be hid; and I shall be a fugitive and a vagabond in the earth; and it shall come to pass, that every one that findeth me shall slay me."*

I can relate to that verse. But God put a mark upon Cain so that he should not be slain. Then Cain went to the land of Noe and built a city. Then another son was born to Adam and Eve, and his name was Seth. This is the line from which Christ came.

Genesis 6:1, 2

"And it came to pass, when men began to multiply on the face of the earth, and daughters were born unto them, that the sons of God saw the daughters of men that they were fair; and they took them wives of all which they chose."

Here in the Bible we find the first examples of a distinction between Lefts and Rights. Sons of God = Rights; spiritual. Daughters of men = Lefts; non-spiritual.

THE FLOOD

There are more than 1.5 million species of animals on the earth today. Countless thousands of them require a very specific environment.

Genesis 9: 1, 9

The third or Noahic covenant: *"And God blessed Noah and his sons, and said unto them, be fruitful, and multiply, and replenish the earth. . . . And I, behold, I establish my covenant with you, and with your seed after you."*

When Noah was drunk, his son Ham looked upon his nakedness, and when Noah awoke he cursed him; drunkenness.

THE TOWER OF BABEL

Genesis 11:7

"Let us go down, and there confound their language that they may not understand one another's speech."

A study of the evolution of the different languages shows without a doubt that many languages developed and were derived in different places on the earth.

I myself have spoken in the "unknown tongue." A spirit used my vocal cords for a few seconds. A man who was with me in my car had been talking profusely. After the spirit spoke, there was complete silence. I did not understand what the spirit said.

Aristotle thought the Greek language was the foundation of all languages. He set up an experiment to prove it. He took twin boys as soon as they were born and isolated them with a woman who was deaf and dumb. They had no communication at all with the outside. Aristotle claimed that the boys started speaking Greek. Modern linguists respond, "Poppycock."

THE FOURTH COVENANT: ABRAHAMIC

Genesis 12:2, 3

God speaks to Abraham: *"And I will make of thee a great nation, and I will bless thee, and make thy name great. And thou shalt be a blessing. . . . And I will bless them that bless thee, and curse them that curseth thee."*

Genesis 13:13

"But the men of Sodom were wicked and sinners before the Lord exceedingly."

Sodomy.

BIRTH OF ISHMAEL

Genesis 16

Because she was old, Sarah gave to Abraham her maid Hagar to have a child, so that the Abrahamic Covenant could be fulfilled. Hagar had a son, Ishmael, but mother and son were cast out when Sarah had Isaac. This is where circumcision started. It results in a circle of flesh—immortality.

Isaac—Father of the Jews.

Ishmael—Father of the Arabs.

Genesis 20

Abraham and Sarah were half brother and sister. Their father was Terah. Incest?

THE OFFERING OF ISAAC

Genesis 22:10

"And Abraham stretched forth his hand, and took the knife to slay his son. And an angel said lay not thine hand upon the lad."

Fear.

Genesis 22:17

"That in blessing I will bless thee, and in multiplying I will multiply thy seed as the stars of the heaven, and as the sand which is upon the sea shore; and thy seed shall possess the gate of his enemies."

This verse makes it quite clear that "God" has promised the world to the Jews and, later, to the Christians. The Christians and Jews are Rights. The world belongs to them. What about the Lefts? Are they busy scratching fleas?

A BRIDE FOR ISAAC

Genesis 24:4

These are the words with which Abraham charged his servants: *"But thou shalt go unto my country, and to my kindred, and take a wife unto my son Isaac."*

Genesis 24:55, 56

"And her brother and her mother said, let the damsel abide with us a few days, at the least ten; after that she shall go. . . . And he said unto them, hinder me not, seeing the Lord hath prospered my way; send me away that I may go to my master."

This borders on kidnapping. In fact there is a very famous painting by Delacroix titled "The Abduction of Rebecca."

Genesis 25:31

When Rebecca bore the twins Esau and Jacob, it was Esau who came out of the womb first. Therefore he deserved the birthright. As an adult, Esau was hungry one day and begged Jacob for a bowl of food he had cooked. Jacob said, "Sell me this day thy birthright." And Esau did. When Isaac was on his deathbed, Jacob deceived his father by pretending to be Esau and stole the blessing.

Is this a case of deceit being rewarded?

Genesis 27:41

"And Esau hated Jacob."

Genesis 29:11

Jacob went to Haran looking for a wife. *"And Jacob kissed Rachel, and lifted up his voice, and wept. And Jacob told Rachel that he was her father's brother, and that he was Rebecca's son."*

Laban had two daughters, Rachel and Leah. An agreement was made between Jacob and Laban that Jacob would work for Laban for seven years in order to win Rachel. Incest again.

But in the wedding tent Laban switched daughters. Deceit again.

Jacob worked seven more years to marry Rachel. Now Jacob had two wives. Polygamy.

Maidens are routinely knocked up in this first book.

Genesis 31:19

"And Laban went to shear his sheep: and Rachel had stolen the images that were her father's."

Thievery.

Genesis 33

The angel with whom Jacob wrestled told Jacob that he would have a new name: Israel.

Genesis 37:3

"Now Israel loved Joseph more than all his children, because he was the son of his old age: And he made him a coat of many colors."

As I have mentioned, my mother made me a coat of many colors when I was young. My father talked incessantly about that coat. Was he jealous, as Joseph's brothers were? Joseph's brothers sold him into slavery. Cruelty.

Joseph and his brothers represent the twelve tribes of Israel. The story of Joseph and his brothers in Egypt is a great story by any standard. At the end of this book Jacob bestows a blessing on each one of his twelve sons.

So the book of Genesis is the story of the creation of the world, not the creation of the earth. It is also the story of the Jews and their relationship with God.

Numbers 22:30

"And the ass said unto Balaam, am not I thine ass, upon which thou hast ridden severe since I was thine unto this day? Was I ever wont to do so unto thee? And he said, nay."

Mr. Ed.

THE PALESTINIAN COVENANT

Deuteronomy 30:5

"And the Lord thy God will bring thee into the land which thy fathers possessed, and thou shalt possess it; and he will do thee good, and multiply thee above thy fathers."

The terms "Lord thy God" and "Lord God" are used extensively in the Bible. They seem to imply that there is more than one God.

Judges 16:30

"And Sampson said, let me die with the Philistines. And he bowed himself with all his might: And the house fell upon the Lords, and upon all the people that were therein."

This is an example of suicide in the Bible.

THE DAVIDIC COVENANT

2 Samuel 7:12

"And when thy days be fulfilled, and thou shalt sleep with thy fathers, I will set up thy seed after thee, which shall proceed out of thy bowels, and I will establish his kingdom."

PSALMS

Psalms 21:10

"Their fruit shalt thou destroy from the earth, and their seed from among the children of men."

To whom does *their* refer?

Psalms 30:3

"O Lord thou hast brought up my soul from the grave: thou hast kept me alive, that I should not go down to the pit."

This is the only possible reason that I am alive.

Psalms 38:12

"They also that seek me after my life lay snares for me; and they that seek my hurt speak mischievous things, and imagine deceits all the day long."

I have only recently realized how evil this world really is. I have had many snares set for me.

Psalms 58:3

"The wicked are estranged from the womb: they go astray as soon as they be born, speaking lies."

I find this hard to believe, unless sanctification is involved.

Psalms 109:5

"And they have rewarded me evil for good, and hatred for my love."

I am sorry to say that those to whom "they" refers are my "friends."

Psalms 137:9

"Happy shall he be, that taketh and dasheth thy little ones against the stones."

This doesn't sound like my God.

Psalms 3:7

"Arise, O Lord; save me, O my God: for thou hast smitten all mine enemies upon the cheek bone; thou hast broken the teeth of the ungodly."

My enemies think this is me because my wives slapped me and I fell and broke my teeth. If my wives could be considered part God (Rights), then this could easily be understood.

Psalms 20:5 and Psalms 60:4

"We will rejoice in thy salvation, and in the name of our God we will set up our banners: The Lord fulfill all thy petitions."

"Thou hast given a banner to them that fear thee, that it may be displayed because of the truth. Selah."

This explains why so many banners are flying from houses today.

Psalms 23:5

"Thou preparest a table before me in the presence of mine enemies: thou anointest my head with oil; my cup runneth over."

Many so-called Christians are thinking this when they are sitting across the table from you.

Psalms 25:19

"Consider mine enemies; for they are many; and they hate me with cruel hatred."

This verse is about me!

Psalms 35:19

"Let not them that are mine enemies wrongfully rejoice over me: neither let them wink with the eye that hate me without a cause."

I have had several experiences with winking.

Psalms 40:14

"Let them be ashamed and confounded together that seek after my soul to destroy it; let them be driven backward and put to shame that wish me evil."

And these are many.

Psalms 115:7

"They have hands, but they handle not: feet have they, but they walk not: neither speak they through their throat."

This could explain the function of the tonsils.

Psalms 118:18

"The Lord hath chastened me sore: but he hath not given me over unto death."

I have suffered much tribulation, barely escaping death many times.

Psalms 141:3

"Set a watch, O Lord, before my mouth; keep the door of my lips."

BLAKE–"A truth that's told with bad intent beats all the lies you can invent."

PROVERBS

Proverbs 3:35

"The wise shall inherit glory: but shame shall be the promotion of fools."

Hints of reincarnation?

Proverbs 14:12

"There is a way which seemeth right unto a man, but the end thereof are the ways of death."

I am sorry to say this, but many good people fall into this trap: spirit versus flesh.

Proverbs 23:32

"At the last it biteth like a serpent, and stingeth like an adder."

Few people quit in time.

Proverbs 24:17

"Rejoice not when thine enemy falleth, and let not thine heart be glad when he stumbleth."

If you rejoice when your enemy falls you are no better than he.

Proverbs 27:1

"Boast not thyself of tomorrow; for thou knowest not what a day may bring forth."

ECCLESIASTES

Ecclesiastes 1:18

"For in much wisdom is much grief: and he that increaseth knowledge increaseth sorrow."

The more you know the more you have to worry about.

Ecclesiastes 10:2

"A wise man's heart is at his right hand; but a fool's heart is at his left."

The right hand refers to the people who are spiritual; the left hand refers to another group of people, those who lack the spirit. This is the pattern all through the Bible: left versus right.

Ecclesiastes 10:20

"Curse not the king, no not in thy thought; and curse not the rich in thy bed chamber: for a bird of the air shall carry the voice, and that which hath wings shall tell the matter."

A book could be written on this verse. When I was a boy I could not understand how my mother knew certain facts. She would say, "A little bird told me." The fact is that spiritual people put thoughts in the brains of others and control their behavior.

PART 2
The Gospels

There are numerous passages from the Old Testament that point to the coming of Christ. In the Gospel of John, the ministry of John the Baptist is foretold. In the Gospels of Matthew and Luke, the genealogy of Christ is written.

Luke 1:30
"Fear not, Mary, for thou hast found favour with God. And behold, thou shalt conceive in thy womb, and bring forth a son and shalt call his name Jesus. He shall be great, and shall be called the son of the most high."

Matthew 1:26
An angel addresses Joseph and says: *"Fear not to take unto thee Mary thy wife: For that which is conceived in her womb is of the Holy Ghost."*

As a biologist, I can state that it is impossible for a human ovum to develop into a viable organism without undergoing a process called fertilization (the union of egg and sperm). There is a process in some lower animals called parthenogenesis, in which the unfertilized egg can begin mitosis without fertilization and produce an offspring. These offspring are all female. For a human female to conceive, however, her ovum must unite with a sperm cell from a male. The resulting cell is called a zygote. It has the full complement of 46 chromosomes, two sets of 23 chromosomes each—one set from the male and one set from the female.

The process by which these egg and sperm cells are formed is called meiosis. In meiosis, cells with two sets of chromosomes end up with only one set of chromosomes: 23. There is a great advantage for organisms to reproduce sexually: great diversity. The reason for this diversity is what is known as "the principle of independent segregation of the chromosomes." Each of a pair of the chromosomes has an equal chance to be in the egg or sperm. The chance of the same set of chromosomes being "chosen" twice is 2^{23}. So you can see where the diversity comes from.

These sperm and egg cells are derived from tissue called germ plasm. There is a theory called "continuity of germ plasm" that states that the purpose of the somatic cells (body) is to protect and pass on the germ cells to the next generation.

The so-called male, or Y chromosomes, and the female, or X chromosomes, are referred to as the sex chromosomes; the other 22 pairs of chromosomes are called the autosomes.

Sex of offspring is determined by which sperm cell fertilizes the egg. If it is a Y sperm, then the offspring will be male, but if it is an X sperm, the offspring will be a female. Females can only produce X chromosomes; the only question is which X.

There are some abnormalities in the numbers of the sex chromosomes such as : (X) (XXX) (XXY) (XYY). The body features are apparent on some of these genotypes. In the prison population, the occurrence of (XYY) is much greater than in the population at large. These men are usually taller than average and usually have a rough complexion. This phenomenon has been used as a defense in some court cases.

I do not doubt that there is such a thing as the Holy Ghost, but I wonder if sometimes he has two legs. This is not meant to take away the spiritual side of the Holy Ghost, but something very physical happened with Mary. Where did the male chromosomes come from? The sperm cell either passed through the abdominal and uterine walls or entered the womb in the conventional way, through the vagina.

The other possibility is that the sperm (with its genes, DNA and very complex biochemistry) was formed inside the womb from nothing. This was truly a miracle.

What is a miracle?

One line of thought states that there is no such thing as a miracle. The fact that events happen for which nobody can find explanation, does not mean that there are no explanations. There are explanations—or reasons—for these events. We just do not understand them.

One definition of a miracle is this: something happening that cannot happen. Another definition is: an extraordinary event manifesting a supernatural work of God. It is obvious that the Christians prefer the latter definition of miracle. If you believe in one miracle, where do you draw the line?

There were spiritual people before Christ. Blake speaks of the brotherhood of Eden. Abraham and his descendants were spiritual people. Jesus gave the spirit not only to Jews, but to everyone.

Mary said, *"As God spake unto our fathers toward Abraham and his seed for ever."*–Luke 1:55

Zacharias said, *"The oath which he swore unto Abraham our Father."*–Luke 1:73

BRADBURY–"And now the rocket, brightest and loudest of all, gives answer and says: I will spread your seed not only here but around the sun in other universal darkness. Where your children's children's children can pass on the original gift of fire first hearthed upon earth.

On that distant day, with all humanity's differences fused by time and multiple effort and the fire of the rocket, itself, mankind with one voice will name us as ancestors, and be glad."

Because we love life and fear death. Man craves immortality.

Matthew 3:10

"And even now is the axe laid unto the root of the trees: every tree therefore that bringeth not forth good fruit is hewn down, and cast into the fire."

This is speaking of Lefts, no doubt.

Matthew 4:1

"Then was Jesus led up of the spirit into the wilderness to be tempted of the devil."

This spirit can easily be understood by anyone who has seen spectres.

John 1:48

"Nathaniel said unto him, whence knowest me? Jesus answered and said unto him: Before Philip called thee, when thou wast under the fig tree, I saw thee."

This could be the result of what Shelley calls: "the awful shadow of some unseen power; that floats through unseen among us."

John 2:5

"Jesus answered, verily, verily, I say unto thee, except a man be born of water and the spirit, he cannot enter into the kingdom of God."

The "born of water" is obviously the physical birth. "Born of the spirit" is another matter. I do not think Lefts can attain this spirit. If God chooses to whom he will give the spirit, the behavior of men is irrelevant. Once I prayed for ten days and ten nights and God saved me. I saw hell. The mechanics of being "born again" is what fascinates me. I understand why, but not how. Maybe no one understands how.

TENNYSON–"I doubt not through the ages one increasing purpose runs, and the thoughts of men are widened with the process of the suns."

John 1:12

"But as many as received him, to them gave he power to become the sons of God, even to them that believe on his name."

This applies to "spiritual" people only; they are as sons of God. Unfortunately, some people are viewed as dogs.

John 4:42

"Now we believe not because of thy speaking; for we have heard for ourselves, and know that this is indeed the savior of the world."

The "world" refers to the spiritual people, otherwise "earth" would have been used.

Matthew 4:19

"And he saith unto them, come ye after me, and I will make you fishers of men."

This topic is covered in Paper One.

Luke 4:35

"And Jesus rebuked him saying hold thy peace, and come out of him. And when the devil had thrown him down in the midst, he came out of him, having done him no hurt."

I once touched a man and a spirit jumped out of his body.

Matthew 12:8

"For the son of man is Lord of the Sabbath."

Here the Christians claim that Jesus was half man and half God. To further confuse things, some Christians claim that Jesus was all God and all man. The fact that Jesus referred to himself as the son of man instead of the son of men means that he had the spirit. He considers men not worthy of mention, at least in this passage.

I heard a sermon once by a preacher who told his congregation that they were like the sons of God.

THE SERMON ON THE MOUNT

The word "blessed" is used often in this sermon. The word "blessed," according to the definition of Webster's Dictionary, could mean praised or cursed.

Luke 6:20

"Blessed are ye poor; for yours is the kingdom of God."

Notice that the present tense is used here.

Luke 19:26

"I say unto you, that unto every one that hath shall be given; but from him that hath not, even that which he hath shall be taken away from him."

Matthew 5:3

"Blessed are the poor in spirit: For theirs is the kingdom of heaven."

The "poor in spirit" refers to the natural man. The present tense, is, means the present. You don't have anything to look forward to after death.

Luke 6:21

"Blessed are ye that weep now: For ye shall laugh."

I am reminded again of an old girlfriend's young daughter who looked at me and said: "You are going to laugh." I was determined not to, but I did. Somehow she controlled my emotions.

Matthew 5:5

"Blessed are the meek: For they shall inherit the earth."

The earth means sphere of mortal life. The earth they will inherit is six feet under.

Matthew 5:6

"Blessed are they that hunger and thirst after righteousness for they shall be filled."

Fed.

Matthew 5:7

"Blessed are the merciful: for they shall obtain mercy."

This does not fit the Christians whom I know. They are ready to hang somebody at the drop of a hat.

WORDS OF JESUS

Matthew 5:13

"Ye are the salt of the earth: but if the salt have lost its savour, wherewith shall it be salted? It is thenceforth good for nothing, but to be cast out, and to be trodden under foot of men."

Here the Lord is speaking about non-spiritual people. When they have lost the savour, or "temper," they are to be cast out and trodden under foot. And many there are.

Matthew 5:15

"Neither do men light a lamp, and put it under a bushel, but on the stand; and it shineth unto all that are in the house."

"All that are in the house" are the Rights.

Matthew 5:20

"For I say unto you, that except your righteousness exceed the righteousness of the scribes and Pharisees, ye shall in no wise enter into the kingdom of heaven."

This righteousness is for the Rights only.

Matthew 5:34

"I say unto you, swear not at all; neither by the heaven, for it is the throne of God; nor by earth, for it is the footstool of his feet."

Here is heaven, the spiritual, and the earth, the non-spiritual.

Matthew 5:44

"But I say unto you love your enemies, and pray for them that persecute you."

I do this often. I wonder if true Christians do this often.

Matthew 6:3

"But when thou doest alms, let not thy left hand know what thy right hand doeth."

Another example of the two types of people, Lefts and Rights. Here is where the term *"Left* out" comes from.

Matthew 7:6

"Give not that which is holy unto the dogs, neither cast ye your pearls before swine, lest they trample them under their feet, and turn again and rend you."

I have seen this verse in action several times. These so-called Christians move their hands like they are casting something before me. The dogs and swine represent the Lefts. My God does not call anybody swine or dogs.

The Rights have "advantage." This is what gives them a feeling of superiority.

Matthew 7:15

"Beware of false prophets, which come to you in sheep's clothing, but inwardly they are ravening wolves."

The world is loaded with them!

Matthew 8:12

"But the sons of the kingdom shall be cast forth into the outer darkness; there shall be weeping and gnashing of teeth."

When I first had my illness, I could hear grinding of teeth. My illness was spiritual.

Matthew 11:14

"And if ye are willing to receive it, this is Elijah, which is to come. He that hath ears to hear, let him hear."

The spirit of Elijah is alive and well.

Luke 7:35

"And wisdom is justified of all her children."

This is the wisdom of the ages, the process of the suns.

Luke 10:21

"In that hour Jesus rejoiced in spirit, and said, I thank thee, O Father, Lord of heaven and earth, that thou hast hid these things from the wise and prudent, and hast revealed them unto babes: even so, Father; for so it seemed good in thy sight."

This is a very important verse. If you are ignorant of the spiritual world you cannot understand this.

Matthew 12:30

"He that is not with me, is against me."

What about the multitude of people who never heard of Christ? Are they condemned to hell?

Mark 3:29

"But whosoever shall blaspheme against the Holy Spirit hath never forgiveness."

This is an attempt to discourage objective study of the Trinity.

Mark 3:35

"For whosoever shall do the will of God, the same is my brother, and sister, and mother."

E Pluribus Unum.

Matthew 13:43

"Then shall the righteous shine forth as the sun in the kingdom of their father."

Shiny faces.

Matthew 9:19

"But when they deliver you up, be not anxious how or what ye shall speak: For it shall be given you in that hour what ye shall speak."

I use this verse.

John 6:43

"Jesus answered and said unto them, murmur not among yourselves. No man can come to me, except the father which sent me draw him."

Here again is an example of God's arbitrarily choosing the people whom he wants to save.

Matthew 9:30

"And their eyes were opened. And Jesus strictly charged them, saying, see that no man know it. But they went forth, and spread abroad his fame in all the land."

I have observed many times Rights telling Lefts not to do certain things while knowing full well that the Lefts are going to do it.

Mark 10:31

"But many that are first shall be last; and the last first."

I've been last all my life.

Matthew 18:18

"What things soever ye shall bind on earth shall be bound in heaven: And what things soever ye shall loose on earth shall be loosed in heaven."

Here is the heaven-earth dichotomy.

Matthew 24:29

"Immediately after the tribulation of those days shall the sun be darkened, and the moon shall not give her light, and the stars shall fall from heaven, and the powers of the heavens shall be shaken."

I have seen pitch dark at noon.

Matthew 25:42, 43

"For I was an hungered, and ye gave me no meat: I was thirsty, and ye gave me no drink: I was a stranger, and ye took me not in: naked, and ye clothed me not: sick, and in prison, and ye visited me not."

This applies to all of my so-called friends. The savour is gone.

John 12:24

"Verily, verily, I say unto you, Except a corn of wheat fall into the ground and die, it abideth alone: but if it die, it bringeth forth much fruit."

The grain of wheat that falls into the ground never dies, but it waits for the right conditions to sprout. It is undergoing a type of respiration known as endogenous metabolism. Some seeds can live for thousands of years.

Mark 9:25

"When Jesus saw that the people came running together, he rebuked the foul spirit, saying unto him, Thou dumb and deaf spirit, I charge thee, come out of him, and enter no more into him."

The majority of people in institutions today are possessed by evil spirits.

Luke 10:24

"Many prophets and kings desired to see the things which ye see, and saw them not: And to hear the things which ye hear, and heard them not."

This seeing and hearing are in another dimension. I have experienced that dimension.

John 15:25

"But this cometh to pass, that the word might be fulfilled that is written in their law, They hated me without a cause."

They hated me! I take this personally.

Luke 12:5

"Be not afraid of them which kill the body, and after that have no more that they can do. But I will warn you whom ye shall fear: Fear him, which after he has killed hath power to cast into hell."

Can Satan also cast into hell? Not according to this verse. What about the pulpit? Who is pulling whom into the pit?

Luke 13:34

"O Jerusalem, Jerusalem, which killeth the prophets, and stoneth them that are sent unto her!"

Here are two types of Jerusalem, the physical and the spiritual.

Luke 15:7

"I say unto you, that even so there shall be joy in heaven over one sinner that repenteth, more than over ninety and nine righteous persons, which need no repentance."

This signifies the conversion of a Right to Christianity, not a Left.

Matthew 14:2

"And straightway ye shall find an ass tied."

The ass that Christ sits upon represents the Lefts.

John 12:43

"For they loved the glory of men more than the glory of God."

I am very conscious of this verse when I do anything. What is my motive?

Matthew 24:29

"And the stars shall fall from heaven."

This statement cannot be, since the stars are infinitely larger than the earth and light years away. The reference could be to meteorites, however, since they are sometimes called shooting stars.

John 14:2

"In my Father's house are many mansions: if it were not so, I would have told you. I go to prepare a place for you."

The mansions are here on earth now. "My Father's House" is heaven, the collections of the souls of spiritual people. Could it be bodies also?

John 15:13

"Greater love hath no man than this, that a man lay down his life for his friends."

I would have done this for my "friends." They would not give me the time of day.

John 20:22

"And when he had said this, he breathed on them, and saith unto them receive ye the Holy Ghost."

This is one way that the spirit can be transferred. Also the resurrected body of Christ has some peculiar properties. At times it appears as flesh and other times as spirit.

John 21:6

"Cast the net on the right side of the boat, and ye shall find."

Right versus Left.

Mark 16:17

"And these signs shall follow them that believe: In my name shall they cast out devils; they shall speak with new tongues."

I have spoken with new tongues, but I have not cast out devils.

Mark 4:12

"That seeing they may see, and not perceive; and hearing they may hear, and not understand; lest at any time they should be converted, and their sins should be forgiven them."

The Rights, or spiritual, see this spiritual truth and also hear it. The "poor in spirit" know nothing.

Mark 4:25

"For he that hath, to him shall be given: and he that hath not, from him shall be taken even that which he hath."

Here is the poor in spirit being fleeced by the Right.

PART 3

Acts and Letters

Acts 2:44-45

"And all that believed were together, and had all things in common; and sold their possessions and goods, and parted them to all men, as every man had need."

Acts 4:32, 35

"And the multitude of them that believed were of one heart and of one soul: neither said any of them that ought of the things which he possessed was his own; but they had all things common. And laid them down at the apostle's feet: and distribution was made unto every man according as he had need."

The *Communist Manifesto* is taken directly from those verses in Acts. The cornerstone of communist philosophy is the phrase, "From each according to his ability, to each according to his needs."

That is one of the most noble thoughts that man could have. Why does it not work? Because there is a fundamental flaw in human nature: greed. The greed of the individual is stronger than the collective greed of the population at large. This could be genetic, for the strongest emotion in man is self-preservation.

What about equal opportunity? Equal opportunity is no more than the chance to be greedy. If a person has food, shelter, clothes, and transportation, what more could he want? It is not greed if a person obtains what he needs. It is greed if a person obtains a vulgar amount of wealth and craves for more.

SHAW–"In my experience the men who want something for nothing are invariably Christians."

God rewards hard work. He will also forgive the unregenerate. He is very patient. He will give you space to repent. If you do not repent he will give you a second time, space to repent. Don't try him a third time.

Acts 17:30

"And the times of this ignorance God winked at; but now commandeth all men everywhere to repent."

ROBBINS–"Who keeps the truth from people stands in the way of God."

This includes most all Rights. Why are they so secretive? If they tell the truth, will the charm be broken? Rights, by and large, hate men. Being a Left, I do not hate the Rights, but I hate their spirits. Nicolaitanes?

REVELATIONS 1:16

"And out of his mouth went a sharp two edged sword."

This two-edged sword is words: metaphors and allegories. Your own words will convict you.

Are Moslems and such Rights? At the end of the six-day war the Jews were negotiating with the Arabs. The Arabs suspected that the Jews could read their minds. I laughed at this at the time, but lately I have realized that this is true. The Christians also have the ability to read minds.

The Jews' ability to read minds and put ideas into the heads of others would seem to make them invulnerable. How, then, did the Holocaust happen? Were the German troops dandies? With their expertise in engineering, I doubt it.

In Florida recently there was a spate of robbing tourists, Germans in particular. A little black boy who was arrested more than sixty times was interviewed on TV. He said, "That money is not theirs, it is mine." I told this to a "friend" of mine and he said, "That's right!" Here we go with the covenants in the Bible again.

LARCOM–"I do not own an inch of land, but all I see is mine."

Is Satan the tempter, or are Christians themselves tempters? A twelve-year-old girl, physically well developed, sat in front of me in church. She wore clothes that were fairly revealing, and several times she would glide past me. I know other Christian females who dress very sexily, too. The Satanic bible also encourages women to dress sexily in order to induce lust.

Here is something else that seems to me to be very peculiar. In the Bible, Christ is symbolized as a lamb. In the Satanic bible, Satan is symbolized as a lamb. Also in the Bible, the devil is referred to as the prince and the power of the air. Air is necessary for sound (speech). Critics of the Bible are not allowed to take sections of it out of context, but preachers are. I am beginning to wonder if Satan has taken over much of Christ's church.

The Satanists believe in killing animals. The Jews also believe in sacrificing animals.

Hebrews 9:22

"And almost all things are by the law purged with blood; and without shedding of blood is no remission of sin."

Why do preachers not preach more on Satan and hell? It is because their motives are very similar. I have observed that Satanists and Christians get along very well together.

Even in the dictionary the Left must read between the lines to receive the true definition. The Rights are a long way from perfect, and it would probably be easier to get rid of the Lefts than to get the Rights to be of one accord.

Call it what you want, but Satan hates me. The ulterior motives of the Christians, being understood by me, are very similar to the motives of the Satanists. Christ will clean house when he returns.

I have some spiritual power. I do not exactly know how much power I have, but I know I have some. The Rights, too, know that I have some power, but they do not know to what extent. The Rights are constantly giving me stimuli to influence my thoughts. No response is also a response.

James 2:19

"Thou believest that there is one God; thou doest well: the devils also believe, and tremble."

In the past two years or so I have observed much trembling in my presence. I have also noticed that when I make a statement, it is so. That immortal sea is the Holy Spirit.

SHELLEY—"The awful shadow of some unseen power; floats through unseen among us."

Somehow the Satanists know people's sins; the Christians know, too. Christians are also engaged in causing people to sin. Where is heaven? Where is hell?

MILTON—"The mind is its own place and in itself can make a heaven of hell, a hell of heaven."

The halos seen over the heads of saints in pictures represent the sun. What about the points of lights that are seen sometimes at night? I have concluded that these points of light are spectres.

Is truth good or evil? I believe that truth could be good or evil; it depends on how it is used. If it is used to help somebody, it is good. If it is used to hurt somebody, it is evil.

Now about lying. Believe me, I am an expert on lying. Why do people lie? I can only draw from my own experience on this matter, but I know this: no behavior occurs without motive. I have reflected on my past lying, and for the most part I would tell others what I thought they wanted to hear. I wanted to please them. Other times, I have lied and told things the way I thought they should be instead of the way they were. This was an attempt to improve on the truth. This is impossible. Artists in the school of expressionism also lie a little bit. They think they can improve on nature.

I have never lied to purposely harm anybody. I know, however, that some lying has subliminal origins. Also, there is lying for self-preservation. There is also lying when a person does not know that he is lying. Blake would say that the mischief is all the same, but I don't believe it.

The Bible is a spiritual book, but the Christians present it as a physical book to Lefts, knowing all the while that the Lefts cannot understand it. There is a series of Christian comic books called the *Crusaders*. The Crusaders of old tried to recapture the Holy Land and kill all of the heathens. This is beginning to sound familiar. (Refer to Gideons.)

In these comic books the policeman, the mayor, and other people in authority are shown as Satanists. These books attempt to undermine the reader's confidence in authority. If a person in tribulation read these books it would put him into double tribulation. These books are not meant to save, but to destroy. They can be purchased at the Christian Book Store.

A "friend" of mine went to a seminary and finished at the top of his class. He was an evangelist for four years. He was at my house and he took a drink of liquor, telling me that it was his first drink in

Confessions of a Dandy

six years. He told me that he had turned down several churches, and I asked him why he got out of preaching. It was obvious to me that he would make a super preacher. He told me that it was not at all as I imagined. He intimated that it was a cut-throat business from the bottom up.

All Rights, be they black or white, enjoy torturing the Lefts. They especially enjoy putting fear into the hearts of Lefts. It is impossible for me to experience fear, however, because it has all been used up. I am not in the least bit afraid of death. If I were, it would make me vulnerable to Satan's fiery darts.

I believe that most behavior is genetic, the spirit notwithstanding. There is just too much evidence to think otherwise. Are female Lefts also dandies? I do not know enough about female Lefts to make a knowledgeable assessment of them. I suspect that they are controlled by the Rights, as are dandies. It is sex that determines our entire life experiences.

The Rights (both black and white) try to short circuit my mind. It does not work. God has given me clarity of thought.

The many times that Rights have borrowed money from Lefts, they never repaid the loans. Now I know that they cannot repay the loans because it would be contrary to their creed. Lefts were made to be taken advantage of in every way. If a Right repaid a Left it would be tantamount to admitting that his creed was flawed.

The Rights are losing power to block my mind. I am gaining power, and no one can do anything about it. I struggled all my life to be normal, but my environment made this impossible. My Cape Horn lasted many years.

Gettysburg is very important. I drove to Gettysburg when I was in tribulation. The car practically drove itself. This leaves me to the term *confederate*. Was the Confederate Army made up largely of Lefts? I cannot believe that the Civil War was fought on the issue of slavery, unless it was chattel slavery. The country was loaded with slaves then, and it is loaded with slaves now—just not as many.

Here is an idea on slavery from Eiseley:

"Intellects talk glibly of psychological 'break-throughs' and the subliminal control of nations. Is it for this that men have labored up the dark pathway behind us and died often and blindly for some vision they could scarcely see?"

The above is the men following the man. More and more, I am beginning to understand that this life must be played by spiritual rules. If a person can kill, except for self-preservation, he can be killed. If a Right wins money from a Left, he must always leave the Left with a little money.

Many of the Rights are in the tribes of Israel. While I by no means know all of the parameters of the spiritual world, God is allowing me some knowledge in this area.

A very bright professor of mine once told me, "About half of what you know is not so." This, spoken to a Left, is easy to understand, since the Left is ignorant of the spiritual world. How did the term *Right* originate as a synonym for "correct"? I think that it is Biblical in origin.

It is much better to trust your heart than your senses. If you are a Left and all that you have to work with is your senses, you are dead.

LUCAS–"The curate thinks you have no soul: I know that he has none."

One of the most difficult tasks that a person could have is looking into himself, being truthful to himself. Many people fool themselves. It is not easy being critical of oneself, but it is an absolute necessity. Most people are afraid of the truth.

Now here is an interesting point. Was the Bible written for dandies as well as for Rights, and of the Rights, only white Rights? I am beginning to understand that neither Christianity nor any major religion was created for the Lefts. How do I know this? This is the only way that the world can be understood. I also can sense it. (No pun intended.)

The more time that passes and the stronger I become, the more ridiculous are the attempts of the Rights to control me. I am becoming more and more a stranger in this world.

THE HOLY BIBLE AND THE SATANIC BIBLE

Satanic bible–"The idea took shape in his head that contrary to what the Christian Bible said, the earth would not be inherited by the meek, but by the mighty."

Holy Bible (Sermon on the Mount)–*"Blessed are the meek: For they shall inherit the earth."*

The Satanists are correct on this one. The earth that the meek will inherit is six feet under. Today the devil is alive and highly popular with a great many people. The Satanic bible outsells the Holy Bible in and around college campuses. It might be noted that "evil" is "live" spelled backwards.

Satanic bible: "We have proved many times over the ninth satanic statement that says the church—and countless individuals—cannot exist without the devil." Here is a statement from the introduction to the Satanic bible: "Satanism is a blatantly selfish, brutal philosophy. . . . For all the centuries of shouting down the devil has received, he has never shouted back at his detractors."

Matthew 5:39

"But I say unto you, that ye resist not evil; but whosoever shall smite thee on thy right cheek, turn to him the other also."

This is not at all like the Christians I know. If someone would smite the Christians that I know on the cheek, they would clean the smiter's clock.

Satanic bible–"If a man smite thee on one cheek, smash him on the other. Is it natural for enemies to do good unto each other?"

Here is an idea about God from the Satanic bible–"The images run from a belief in a God who is some vague sort of universal cosmic mind to an anthropomorphic deity with a long white beard and sandals who keeps track of every action of each individual."

According to the Satanic bible the seven deadly sins of the Christian Church are: greed, pride, envy, anger, gluttony, lust, and sloth. The Satanists believe in committing all of these sins. I have noticed that the Christians commit most of these sins themselves. I could write much about the seven deadly sins, but if you are interested in them, buy a Satanic bible.

Now about languages. I don't believe I can accept the Tower of Babel as the only cause of diverse tongues. Satanic bible: "Masses which had been said in Latin are now said in native languages—which only succeeds in making the nonsense easier to understand." (Neither Protestants nor Satanists have much use for the Catholic Church.)

I have heard much speaking in tongues in certain churches. I have also heard Satanists speak in tongues. Enochian is the official language of the Satanists. Some sources claim that Enochian is as old as Sanskrit. I believe that Latin may also play a part in tongues.

Satanism is the only religion known to man that accepts man as he is and promotes the rationale of turning a bad thing into a good thing rather than bending over backward to eliminate the bad thing. Pious prophets have taught man to fear Satan. But what of terms like "God fearing"? If God is so merciful, why do people have to fear him? I'll tell you why. God—not Satan—has the keys to death and to hell.

Revelation 1:18

"I am he that liveth, and was dead; and, behold I am alive for evermore, amen; and have the keys of hell and of death."

Here is a trap which many very religious people fall into. Satanic bible: "Every pharisaic religionist claims to love his enemies, even though when wronged, he consoles himself by thinking: 'God will punish them.'

Here is a statement in the Satanic bible which I think is true. I can draw from my own experience: "Asexuals are invariably sexually sublimated by their jobs or hobbies."

Here is something on psychic vampires: "but he will hasten to add that *you* fulfill every requirement and are truly an outstanding exception among men—you are one of the very few worthy of his friendship."

Here is something from the Satanic bible on human sacrifice–"The only time a Satanist would perform a human sacrifice would be if it were to serve a two-fold purpose: that being to release the magician's wrath in the throwing of a curse, and more important to dispose of a totally obnoxious and deserving individual."

It would not be fitting to finish this section without a comment on money from the Satanic bible–"If the rich man's entry into heaven seems as difficult as the camel's attempt to go through the eye of a needle; if the love of money is the root of all evil; then we must at least assume the most powerful men on earth to be the most Satanic."

Here is something on curses from the Satanic bible–"The most receptive victims of curses have always been the greatest scoffers . . . but the victim of a hex or curse is much more prone to destruction if he does not believe in it." I can relate to that. The fact that nobody knows everything leaves a little space for the unknown. This unknown space is where the spirits take over. It matters not how intelligent the person is.

Satanic bible–"It matters not whether anyone attaches any significance to your working, so long as the results of the working are in accordance with your will. The super-logician will always explain the connection of the magical ritual to the end result as 'coincidence'."

The man who sold me the Satanic bible told me that it was mostly bullshit. However, I have discovered some truth in the Satanic bible. There is just enough truth in it to give it some plausibility. The man was right about the bullshit.

ROMANS

Romans 3:10

"As it is written, there is none righteous, no not one."

This and several more verses in this book seem to imply that this book was written primarily for the Rights, both black and white, both saved and unsaved.

Romans 4:13

"For the promise, that he should be the heir of the world, was not to Abraham, or to his seed, through the law, but through the righteousness of faith."

This verse completely omits the Lefts. It pertains to Rights, both black and white.

Romans 8:14

"For as many as are led by the spirit of God, they are the sons of God."

I do not believe that a non-spiritual person can attain this spirituality as things stand. Here is a quotation from Adams: "Friends are born, not made."

Romans 9:15

"For he saith to Moses, I will have mercy on whom I will have mercy, and I will have compassion on whom I will have compassion."

According to this verse you just have to be lucky to be a Right and unlucky to be a Left.

Romans 12:5

"So we, being many are one body in Christ, and every one members one of another."

Ol' E Pluribus Unum again.

My being the only dandy in my high school class leads me to believe that dandies, especially old dandies, are very rare. It is very lonesome being an old dandy. I know that I am separated from the Rights by spiritual means. The Rights have one another to lean on, while I have only God to lean on. My only true friend is God.

When I was in great tribulation at my father's house, I wanted desperately to become a Christian. I prayed the sinner's prayer as sincerely as anyone has ever prayed the sinner's prayer, to no avail. Two spirits did enter my mind, and they are as mysterious today as they were the day that I received them. I tried to become a Christian harder than anyone has ever tried to become a Christian.

I wrote the papers which are presented in this book, not to criticize God, but to try to understand Him better. I am beginning to wonder whether or not the Christians have a monopoly on God. The Christians think they do.

I believe in a God that is not like other people's God. At least, I view him differently than other people. The more God reveals to me, the more I must write. In other words, I am doing God's work. God has sanctioned these papers—this book—mistakes and all. The mistakes that I have made are to remind me that I am human.

God has also allowed me to synthesize thoughts. That is, to put two or more thoughts together and devise a new way of thinking.

With a decline in the number of dandies there is also a decline in the amount of money received from the dandies by the Rights. In other words, the suckers are becoming rare!

Matthew 5:13

"Ye are the salt of the earth: But if the salt have lost its savour, wherewith shall it be salted? It is thenceforth good for nothing, but to be cast out, and to be trodden under foot of men."

The Sermon on the Mount is a good example of the great dichotomy which pervades the Bible. I have heard all my life that so-and-so is the salt of the earth, that is, he is a very good person. In reality, the salt of the earth is a dandy. Since I am a dandy—and more, a spiritual dandy—I can understand the Sermon on the Mount very well.

My life parallels the typical life of a dandy except for one thing: I am still alive in my old age. Some dandies are quite intelligent and talented in their youth, but when they begin to decline physically and mentally they are like the salt that has lost its taste—to be cast out and to be trodden under foot by men.

The dandy is the natural man. The Rights, with their spiritual world, drive the typical dandy insane. Most dandies are driven to suicide or are killed. Since the spiritual world controls the five senses, a dandy is helpless if that is all that he has to work with. God has given me, a dandy, spiritual knowledge; this makes most Rights very uneasy.

1 Peter 4:12

"Beloved, think it not strange concerning the fiery trial which is to try you, as though some strange thing happened unto you."

I have passed this test.

John 3:16

"For God so loved the world, that he gave his only begotten son, that whosoever believeth in him should not perish, but have everlasting life."

This oft quoted verse seems to be contradicted by the following verse.

1 John 2:15

"Love not the world, neither the things that are in the world. If any man love the world, the love of the father is not in him."

Why is it that the father loves the world so much but instructs the Christians not to love the world? The Christians whom I know love the world very much.

It may be noted that some sort of religion is very important. A religion fills the blank space in a person's psyche. That blank space in a person's psyche will end up killing a person if it is not filled with a workable philosophy or religion.

I have long marveled at the gargoyles on the ancient cathedrals of Europe. The gargoyles are half man, half beast. The Gargoyles are half Rights, half Lefts. Also, the gargoyles are made to frighten the Lefts.

Both Christians and Satanists try to confuse me. They are losing power and I am gaining power. As far as I can see, the whole lot are in the synagogue of Satan.

It is significant that Christians and Satanists have the ability to put fear into the hearts of dandies. I do not know the mechanics of this, but it has been worked on me many times. I don't believe that Christ meant for the spirit to be used in this manner.

Through observation, I have perceived that the Rights are afraid of me. They know that God protects me. He will continue to protect me as long as I do his will.

Revelation 2:10

"Be thou faithful unto death, and I will give thee a crown of life."

An old friend of mine told me years ago that he was afraid to go to church. What exactly goes on in church to cause a brave man to be afraid?

In the latter days strange things will happen.

2 Peter 3:3

"Knowing this first, that there shall come in the last days scoffers, walking after their own lusts."

The thoughts I have set down are being scoffed at by some people, but in the end it is the power in this book that will do the scoffing. It is much like the Judo expert who uses his opponent's strength to defeat him.

At death, where do the souls go? The souls of the Rights, both black and white, are different from the souls of the dandies. The souls of Rights, I know, are somehow transferred to the bodies of living Rights. Does this transfer take place at the time of death? Does this transfer occur before death? Does a human zygote have a soul? If it does, where does the soul come from? I hate to admit it, being a dandy, but I believe dandies are programmed for hell. Not this dandy, however. A Satanist told me many years ago that I was different from other people, and I am. The dandies are sold out, by the Rights, to Satan.

When I was a young boy, I was forced to go to church every time the doors opened—literally, thousands of times. I did not understand this "born again" and "Jesus loves me." I did not understand it then, and I do not understand it now. However, the term "born again" is becoming a little clearer.

My father has not given up yet. He is continually giving me calendars and tracts with religious overtones. I have read many of the papers he has given me, and they all draw a blank. If you tell me something that I do not understand, then it is not true as far as I am concerned. It is deception. Maybe these tracts are too trite for me to understand, or maybe they are over my head. Maybe I am not spiritual enough to understand them. My father knows this, but he continues to give them to me. As I ponder over why he does this, I know that no behavior occurs without motive. The only motive that I can suppose is a feeble attempt at confusion. Satan is the author of confusion.

You cannot cheat in life and get away with it. I tried to cheat in life numerous times in the past. Each time that I cheated I was repaid many times over.

Satan has only what God allows him to have. All energy comes from God.

How do the Rights obtain the knowledge that is in the mind of the dandy? They know that which is in the conscious mind and the unconscious mind. I could write a book on this concept.

Confessions of a Dandy

If there is a bank that contains all of the thoughts of each individual, who does the judging on judgment day? God or Satan? This bank is in the fourth dimension: the spiritual.

Jesus told the woman at the well everything that she had done. Can the Christians of today duplicate that feat? How about the Satanists? Can they duplicate that feat? Can both Christians and Satanists duplicate that feat?

I observed my father in white. He was in the sun and was exceeding white as snow—transfiguration. The devil is also an angel of light. Know this: for everything that God has, Satan has a counterfeit.

Satanists and Christians both put pressure on me, and I cannot tell the difference. I must conclude that the white and black Rights cooperate with one another. Christ is not the problem, it is how Christianity is used that is the problem. I am getting closer to the truth. A lot of little truths add up to the one big truth.

Many of my "friends" and family desire that I work on my music again. This would take me away from my first love, which is the pursuit of truth. I will play the piano only when, and if, God tells me to. I am no longer a "meek."

KENNEDY–"The meek, the terrible meek, the fierce agonizing meek, are about to enter into their inheritance."

Now, it does not take a Shakespeare to realize what the inheritance of the meek is: hell! This leads me to a question. Can Lefts be saved? If Lefts cannot be saved, I am going to be the first one to defy that rule and be saved.

The hope of the Rights is eternal slavery for the dandies, as well as immortality for themselves. The Rights cannot use the knowledge they gain by spiritual means unless the physical barrier is broken.

Sometimes when I am alone, I do some thinking that may best be termed as wild speculation. This leads to some incredible connections. These connections sometimes lead to the truth. There can be no doubt that God is protecting me, even though the Christians and Satanists are allied against me.

Are there two E Pluribus Unums—one for the white Rights and another for the black Rights? This is a part of the great dichotomy. The great dichotomy is the Rights, spiritual, and the Lefts, physical.

Are the minds of the Rights functional units by themselves, or do they depend on all other units? Are they all connected to the Holy Spirit, which some people call the body of Christ? Distance means little when it comes to the spirit. I suspect that spirits can travel at the speed of light, and cannot rule out faster than the speed of light. Of course, the Holy Spirit pervades the whole world.

How about the modern guilds and the guilds of old? The guilds are made up of tradesmen, including such groups as brick masons, carpenters, plumbers, and tailors. They all must not only be skilled tradesmen, but must be Rights.

There are some thoughts that the Rights cannot monitor. These may be termed as spontaneous thoughts. The thoughts that they can monitor are the thoughts that they have put into my mind, and those are considerable.

Now, I would like to say something about curses. The Satanists strongly believe in the effectiveness of curses. Being on the receiving end of many of those curses, I can say that there is some substance to them. The Satanists who throw curses must have an image—such as a photograph or a piece of clothing—of the person who is being cursed—then destroy it. This begins the curse. Here is something strange: I believe Christians are over their heads in this curse-throwing business. If a person is strong enough spiritually, the curses do not work. They bounce back to the sender. Here is what quenches all of the fiery darts: love. Love conquers all.

The possession of spirits is something that has aroused my curiosity for years. All spiritual people are aware of this situation, although most will deny it. The Bible is loaded with accounts of people who are possessed with spirits, demons, or what have you. How about the possessing of people today by spirits? I believe that the majority of people in mental institutions are possessed by spirits. It may be true that some have a chemical imbalance in their brain. The energy that runs the brain, as well as the rest of the body, is electrochemical. What is the relationship between this electrical energy and the spirits? Are spirits some type of electrical field?

How do Satanists attain eternal life? This I do not know, unless it is the same way that Christians do.

An open mind is very important while studying the spiritual world. There must be no preconceived notions. With objective reasoning I have discovered that many of my fundamental beliefs are flawed. The spiritual world can only be understood by spiritual means.

I know for a fact that some Satanists attend church. I believe that many Satanists are church members.

An old "friend" told me, "If you look for good in a person you can find it, and if you look for evil in a person you can find that also."

Confessions of a Dandy

Here is an example of the creed of Rights as it relates to a Left (me). I must take much medication. I received a druggist's statement that overcharged me by more than a hundred dollars. I had a paper from the insurance company that proved his statement wrong. He told me to give him the paper, and I did. He walked away and when he returned he did not have my insurance papers. I asked him where they were and he said that I didn't give him any papers. He said that he didn't know what I was talking about. This is just one example of the creed of the Rights giving a Left, me, the shaft. The druggist felt that he had to cheat me. It was part of his creed.

There was a severely mentally ill man in the town where I grew up. There was another man who picked on him. When I became mentally ill and very depressed he picked on me, also. That behavior must be in his creed.

For years I thought that my experience down at Silly's was a very rare occurrence. Since then I have realized that it was closer to the rule than I ever imagined. I was living in a dream world. I did not realize the danger in anything.

I could be wrong, but it appears to me that the black Rights have as much power as the white Rights. Where is this bank of knowledge that is available to the Rights? As I previously mentioned, it may be the Holy Spirit.

Something that I have noticed many times is this: people, when talking to me, stare at an area above the top of my head. The existence and importance of this place is supported in English literature, in Blake's work in particular. Halos are also located in this place. I have personally observed lights over certain people's heads.

In these papers I have been truthful, but not completely truthful. I am protecting the ones I love. Future papers I write will be more and more truthful and will gradually form closure.

1 CORINTHIANS

1 Corinthians 1:27

"But God hath chosen the foolish things of the world to confound the wise; and God hath chosen the weak things of the world to confound the things which are mighty."

Here I am, foolish and weak.

1 Corinthians 2:7

"But we speak the wisdom of God in a mystery, even the hidden wisdom, which God ordained before the world unto our glory."

Glory is one of an infinite number of reincarnations.

1 Corinthians 2:14

"But the natural man receiveth not the things of the Spirit of God: for they are foolishness unto him: neither can he know them, because they are spiritually discerned."

I rest my case: spirit versus unspirit.

1 Corinthians 3:16

"Know ye not that ye are the temple of God, and that the Spirit of God dwelleth in you?"

This is the kingdom of God: the spirit.

1 Corinthians 15:22

"For as in Adam all die, even so in Christ shall all be made alive."

Reincarnation again.

1 Corinthians 15:40

"There are also celestial bodies, and bodies terrestrial: but the glory of the celestial is one, and the glory of the terrestrial is another."

Body or soul.

1 Corinthians 15:51

"Behold, I shew you a mystery; We shall not all sleep, but we shall all be changed."

This could be where a soul is transferred. The last trump is not necessarily a trumpet.

2 Corinthians

2 Corinthians 3:18

"But we all, with open face beholding as in a glass the glory of the Lord, are changed into the same image from glory to glory, even as by the Spirit of the Lord."

The Bible: from glory to glory
The Koran: from state to state
All major religions are based on reincarnation. Most also believe in sun worship and human sacrifice.

2 Corinthians 4:7

"But we have this treasure in earthen vessels, that the excellency of the power may be of God, and not of us."

Earthen vessels are bodies. The treasure is the soul.

2 Corinthians 4:18

"While we look not at the things which are seen, but at the things which are not seen: for the things which are seen are temporal; but the things which are not seen are eternal."

This is impossible for a Left person to understand.

2 Corinthians 11:12

"But what I do, that I will do, that I may cut off occasion from them which desire occasion; that wherein they glory, they may be found even as we."

These are the Lefts that Paul cuts off.

2 Corinthians 11:14

"And no marvel; for Satan himself is transformed into an angel of light."

I have observed Satan as an angel of light.

Why do some men and most women suffer from herpephobia, the fear of snakes? Could it have biblical implications? The original sin, in which the serpent caused Adam and Eve to disobey God, may be at the root of this irrational fear. Spiritual descendence instead of genetics is probably the reason.

Cain and Abel. It has never been explained to my satisfaction why God accepted Abel's sacrifice and rejected Cain's. Does God require an animal sacrifice? Satan does.

I am beginning to realize that everything is spiritual. Even the abiotic environment is spiritual.

There are several sources possible for the wisdom in this book. One possibility is that these papers are inspired by God. Another possibility is that they are inspired by Satan. The other possibility is that I wrote them without any supernatural help.

My mother told me many times that the worse people treated me, the better I liked them. This was true, because I had no frame of reference. I had been mistreated from birth and knew nothing but ill treatment. Of course, the creeds come into play here. If something good happens to a dandy, it is viewed by the Rights as evil, but if something evil happens to a dandy, it is viewed as good.

Why did God choose me to write the papers that form this book? I must be the biggest dandy in the world. I may be scheduled to bust hell wide open. People don't tell me anything; God reveals things to me. I am doing something that Rights would not dare to do. They cannot stand the truth and cannot stand a dandy knowing the truth.

I truly did not want to believe that the spiritual world existed, but God has shown it to me an infinite number of times. Can a dandy be responsible for his behavior if he is spiritually controlled by Rights? English literature has much to say about unrequited love, that is, love that is given and not returned. My love was never returned.

When I was a little boy of about five, I had a habit of twisting my hair. My mother would discipline me for such behavior. Then, in a few minutes, I would be twisting my hair again. I don't need to describe what was taking place here.

Sometimes I talk to God. I know that the Rights have a tremendous advantage over me, but I call it, simply, that: advantage. I have not asked God for advantage over the Rights, only a level playing field. I have asked him to either take away the advantage of the Rights or to give me the same advantage that they have.

I drink coffee every morning with two men whom I dearly love. One of them is my father. Our conversation can be described as banter, but deeper down it is a war of wits. I can relax around these two men. I don't—won't—think it, but there must be ulterior motives. There is something else going on here and in my conversations elsewhere. I can get bits and pieces of the English language, but I can't quite put it together. Also there is a lot of clearing of the throat. I don't know whether this throat clearing is a signal for me to begin speaking or for me to pay attention because someone is ready to speak.

This brings me to a comment on the tonsils and the adenoids. Mine were removed when I was five years old. Having been trained in biology, I should be familiar with the structure and function of these organs. In textbooks the functions are never mentioned, and the structure is usually vague—such as masses of lymphoid tissue in the throat. If these structures were vestigial organs, they must have had an important function in ages past. Recently I read one possible function of the tonsils (which I consider ridiculous). It is simply this: the tonsils are to keep infections from going deeper in the body and keep them where they can easily be treated. Here is the real function: one sends and the other receives.

Christianity is a religion despite what Christians say: "Religion will send you to hell." The definition of religion is this: "A belief in spiritual beings."

Christians will tell you this, and it is true: the religious leaders, Pharisees, crucified Christ.

How about the second coming of Christ? The Christians say that he will be accepted on his second coming. I don't believe it. I believe the religious people of today are no different from the religious people of two thousand years ago. They will try to crucify Christ again, but with a very different outcome.

TENNYSON—"There lies more faith in honest doubt, believe me, than in all your creeds."

In all honesty, I must include information concerning my good "friend" Lunnie. He has cheated me out of much money through the years, in addition to attempting to take my life several times. I did not know that my being a dandy pertained to our relationship, but it must.

TENNYSON—"He that wrongs his friend wrongs himself more, and ever bears about a silent court of justice in his breast, himself the judge and jury, and himself the prisoner at the bar, ever condemned."

One thing that helps explain my situation is an understanding of the state. It is hard to bite the hand that feeds me, but truth must prevail. The state is also a spiritual condition. I worked very hard for the state for nine years. As circumstances arose, the state caused me to become insane. I deserve my pension.

Masons. About two hundred years ago the Masons were referred to as Free Masons. This denoted that the minds of the Masons were free. Many Christians believe that the Masons are Satanic. It is true that they are very powerful. I suspect that they sacrifice some animals. This is to satisfy their god. Maybe in some cases Satan is worshipped as God.

When I first entered tribulation, I went from church to church trying to find the truth. I found no support in the churches, whatsoever. Quite the contrary, I found mental and spiritual torture. From the beginning, I sensed that my problem was spiritual. I truly believe that the Christians do not want me to become a Christian. They want me to become a scapegoat. They really and truly think that I am evil, when the opposite is true.

My TV exploded one night. The TV was a major source of subliminal messages sent to me, especially the blips. I ask myself what is the benefit of watching TV, knowing that no behavior occurs (regardless of how irrational) without motive. Here are the programs I watch: *The Price Is Right*, all of the news programs, and *Jeopardy*.

The news and *Jeopardy* can be quite informative. I watch the news and *Jeopardy* because they are beneficial to me; they bring me information. With *The Price Is Right*, I can put my mind in neutral and relax. I will admit that, other than this, it is a wasted hour.

Several places in the Bible it is written that God is no respector of persons. What does this mean? I believe that this statement is meant exclusively for the Rights, and, possibly, for only the white Rights. One soul is no more important than another. It could refer to the dandies, but I don't believe it.

When I was about twelve years old, I was down at my grandfather's office when a very strange man entered. He was a huge man (not fat) and was dressed in black. My grandfather and the man in black stood beside one another. They were communicating, but I could not quite understand it. Suddenly, the man in black turned and walked toward the back of the office, where there was no exit. There was a loud clack and the man disappeared. The clack was caused by air columns coming together, much like thunder. Dematerialization.

Now, I saw and heard this, but it barely registered in my mind. Why? Because to me it seemed as though this was impossible. It was a miracle. Does a miracle have to be good?

Feelings. Since the Rights are half spiritual and half physical, then they should only sense half of the pain. As I have written before, the Rights also can derive some pleasure out of causing pain in a dandy. It will suffice to say that this is true. I don't want to go off on a tangent.

I mentioned this before, but I feel that I must address it again: friendship. I feel as though people must pretend when they are nice to me, for I know they hate me.

MILTON–"For who can think submission? War, then, war open or understood must be resolved."

What about truth versus faith? In the sixteenth century a scientist named Galileo invented the telescope. Turning this new invention toward the heavens, he discovered the moons of Jupiter (the four largest moons, still referred to today as the Galilean moons). In addition, he observed sunspots and craters on the moon, and devised a system that could explain the peculiar motion of certain stars (planets). He declared that this could be understood if the sun were the center of the universe, i.e., that earth is part of a solar system.

The Catholic Church pronounced this to be heresy and threatened Galileo with torture if he didn't recant. They showed

Confessions of a Dandy

him the torture chamber but did not use it on him. They placed him under house arrest and instructed him to write no more papers. The official belief of the church was that the earth, not the sun, was the center of the universe. Evidently the church believed that faith was more important than truth. Incidentally, in 1996 the Pope pardoned Galileo—four hundred years too late.

There was an old philosopher named Trismegistus who stated that the sun was the visible part of God. Sophocles said that the sun is all-seeing.

God is a spirit. How many spirits are there? If God is a spirit, how can a non-spiritual person understand him? Is God an electrical field?

Why is the United States so powerful? I believe the reason lies in the spiritual condition of this country. The ratio of Rights in this country is greater than the ratio of Rights in other countries. The reason could be deeper than this, but I will not speculate.

Jews and Christians are spiritually the same thing. I suspect that the Christians, at least some of them, have adopted some of the tribes of the Jews. Halie Salasie of Ethiopia claimed that he and his clan were descended from Juda. He was referred to as "The Lion of Juda." The Christians and Jews both claim to be descended from Abraham—the Jews, spiritually and genetically, the Christians, spiritually.

Which is more important, the spirit or genetics? I believe the spirit, when applied to man.

I must mention the Holocaust. How could this happen to God's chosen people? I can only conclude that it was some kind of sacrifice. If the Jews had the spirit of God with them, they would be impervious to any danger. I have also noticed that there is great variation among the Rights.

Are there degrees in believing? Are there degrees in truth? The Greeks have the apreoric truth, which is eternal truth (mathematics). Many people believe that heaven and hell are graduated. A person is rewarded or punished according to (if you please) his Karma.

I believe that habits are spiritual. Habits are a result of what I call mind-set. A strong willed person can break a habit by changing his mind-set. I consider myself a strong willed person and, as an example, I will use that old bugaboo, smoking. If I decide to smoke, there is nothing that can keep me from smoking. If I decide not to smoke, I have a strong enough mind-set to abstain.

The law was not made for the righteous (Right) man, but for the unrighteous (Left). There is no way that any person can keep all of the spiritual laws, and if he breaks one, he is guilty of breaking them all. This reminds me of the "code of military conduct." Article 23 states that a soldier can be disciplined for "conduct unbecoming a soldier"—the catch-all article.

Let me mention the evil done to dandies. It was the creed of the Rights that was responsible. Is there no justice? If you tell a person evil about yourself, he will believe even worse. But if you tell a person good about yourself, he will not believe it at all.

All of my past experiences have been necessary in order for me to find the ultimate truth. Most people do not believe that there is such a thing as absolute knowledge; I do. His name is God!

There is also, to no one's surprise, a spiritual aspect to games. Once I was playing "Jeopardy" with a friend of mine (a Ph.D.) A girl played the host, and each of us had a clicker. When she asked a question, even if I clicked first, she would recognize the Ph.D. first. He beat me even in categories that were in my areas of expertise. I knew that something strange was happening, but I could not put my finger on it. The fact is, he was obtaining information from my mind—mind reading, if you please.

I ask if there is something going on with the TV *Jeopardy*, which is over my head.

About half of the people in the country, myself included, believe that UFOs really exist. If beings were ten million years more advanced that we humans are, they could have unimagined powers. Ten million years is only a blink when compared to eternity.

Some people believe that Jesus is a spaceman. Here is something of which you can rest assured: even aliens must obey God. The true God is not only the God of this world, but the God of the universe. I believe I have had experiences with aliens several times. The point in time when the spirit entered *Homo erectus* is when *Homo erectus* became *Homo sapiens*. Adam? Abraham? Christ? Some of these stories of the Old Testament are not so far fetched if the spiritual aspects are considered.

Man himself is a hybrid: half spirit, half man. The Rights consider themselves half God, half man. I am worthy because I realize that I am the most unworthy. No conceit.

It is impossible for Rights to be truthful to me for this reason: if the secrets are revealed, the charms will be broken.

Parker writes this: "A Democracy is the idea of freedom." There can be no true democracy while chattel slavery exists— dandies.

There is a method by which the Rights can cause me to forget what I am speaking about. Many people who have encountered aliens speak of having amnesia induced by the aliens. My mind is becoming stronger. I know that my mother can sense my presence. She can also see through my eyes. I know this as fact.

MEREDITH–"His art can take the eyes from out my head, until I see with eyes of other men."

I can also sense when the Rights attempt to put pressure on me. I cannot tell whether it is the white Rights, Christians, or the black Rights, Satanists. The mischief is all the same.

You ask me, "What is the future of the dandies?" The Rights better study up, because it may be their future.

Abraham's spiritual descendants are gradually crowding out the dandies. How long will this last? It may be like the string which fences in the sheep in *Animal Farm*.

This must be included in this book: they hate me without a cause. They also tried to make me evil, with some success. The creed of the Rights makes it necessary to have somebody or something to hate, a scapegoat.

Sometimes when I make a statement to people they wince. I don't understand the motive behind this behavior, but there must be one.

I believe that God can turn a person over to Satan. This is Biblical. It is almost as if Satan is God's "leg man." I am beginning to suspect that Satan is impersonating Christ. Why do we not hear more about Satan, when he is everywhere? Satan is the one who put me into the insane asylum.

At one time I needed someone to lean on. I got no one. Now I do not need any one to lean on. Quite the contrary, I am now powerful enough to allow other people to lean on me. I am the opposite of a psychic leach.

Some people are beginning to treat me better. Is the motive for this that they like me, or is the motive for this that they fear me?

The system does not work for me. I fell through the cracks. I must change or the system must change. The deck is stacked against dandies. We need a new deck.

PART 4

Mostly Paul

Galatians 4:30

"Nevertheless what saith the scripture? Cast out the bondwoman and her son: for the son of the bondwoman shall not be heir with the son of the freewoman."

This speaks of Isaac and Ishmael. Ishmael represents the Lefts.

Galatians 6:7

"Be not deceived; God is not mocked: for whatsoever a man soweth, that shall he also reap."

This one will backfire on some Rights.

Ephesians 6:12

"For we wrestle not against flesh and blood, but against principalities, against powers, against the rulers of the darkness of this world, against spiritual wickedness in high places."

This spiritual wickedness is everywhere, even at the top.

Philippians 4:11

"Not that I speak in respect of want: for I have learned, in whatsoever state I am, therewith to be content."

I live by this precept.

Colossians 3:9

"Lie not one to another, seeing that ye have put off the old man with his deeds."

This does not include the Lefts.

1 Thessalonians 4:6

"That no man go beyond and defraud his brother in any matter: because that the Lord is the avenger of all such, as we also have forewarned you and testified."

This applies to the Right. The word "brother" gives it away.

1 Thessalonians 4:17

"Then we which are alive and remain shall be caught up together with them in the clouds, to meet the Lord in the air: and so shall we ever be with the Lord."

This is easy to believe if you have ever seen spectres.

2 Thessalonians 1:6

"Seeing it is a righteous thing with God to recompense tribulation to them that trouble you . . ."

This verse works well for me.

1 Timothy 1:13

"Who was before a blasphemer, and a persecutor, and injurious: but I obtained mercy, because I did it ignorantly in unbelief."

I did most of my sinning in ignorance.

1 Timothy 6:10

"For the love of money is the root of all evil: which while some coveted after, they have erred from the faith, and pierced themselves through with many sorrows."

Most recovering alcoholics either turn to God or money. This is almost invariably true.

1 Timothy 6:20

"O Timothy, keep that which is committed to thy trust, avoiding profane and vain babblings, and oppositions of science falsely so called."

Modern day science includes the study of the spiritual world. Dr. Rhyne, at Duke University, pioneered in the field of parapsychology.

2 Timothy 3:1

"This know also, that in the last days perilous times shall come."

These perilous times are here today.

Hebrews 4:12

"For the word of God is quick, and powerful, and sharper than any two-edged sword, piercing even to the dividing asunder of soul and spirit, and of the joints and marrow, and is a discerner of the thoughts and intents of the heart."

I have used a two-edged sword at times. It is an expression that can be taken more than one way.

Hebrews 11:1

"Now faith is the substance of things hoped for, the evidence of things not seen."

The things hoped for are reincarnation of the spirit.

James 1:19

"Wherefore, my beloved brethren, let every man be swift to hear, slow to speak, slow to wrath."

Very good advice to *everybody*.

James 2:10

"For whosoever shall keep the whole law, and yet offend in one point, he is guilty of all."

Many Christians break laws that they don't think are important and criticize people that do not keep all the laws. Remove the beam from your eye.

James 2:19

"Thou believest that there is one God; thou doest well: the devils also believe, and tremble."

I have seen many people tremble around me. However, I certainly don't claim to be God.

James 4:7

"Submit yourselves therefore to God. Resist the devil, and he will flee from you."

The stronger the spirit becomes, the truer this verse is.

James 4:17

"Therefore to him that knoweth to do good, and doeth it not, to him it is sin."

This does not count where Lefts are concerned.

1 Peter 4:7

"But the end of all things is at hand: be ye therefore sober, and watch unto prayer."

I believe this.

1 Peter 5:9

"Whom resist stedfast in the faith, knowing that the same afflictions are accomplished in your brethren that are in the world."

I have a very strong feeling that I have some brothers somewhere.

2 Peter 1:14

"Knowing that shortly I must put off this my tabernacle, even as our Lord Jesus Christ hath shewed me."

Peter knows his soul is sanctified.

1 John 2:15

"Love not the world, neither the things that are in the world. If any man love the world, the love of the Father is not in him."

BLAKE–"Since all the riches of the world may be gifts from the devil and earthly kings, I should suspect that I worshipped the devil if I thanked my God for worldly things."

1 John 4:18

"There is no fear in love; but perfect love casteth out fear: because fear hath torment. He that feareth is not made perfect in love."

All my life, off and on, I have been unsure and afraid. Now, I fear absolutely nothing.

Jude 1:16

"These are murmurers, complainers, walking after their own lusts; and their mouth speaketh great swelling words, having men's persons in admiration because of advantage."

Spiritual people use this "advantage" to subject nonspiritual people in every way.

You must love yourself more than you hate yourself, or be killed. The hate that a Right may have for a dandy is balanced by fear, fear of the dandy? No! Fear of God. The Rights rely on fear as their major weapon. I am beginning to think that the Rights themselves have something to fear. The Rights hate the dandy, not the spirit of the dandy. I sometimes hate the spirits of the Rights, and I am convinced that some of these spirits are Satanic. I would much rather have Satan after me than God after me.

About two years ago, I told my good "friend" Lunnie that before I became disabled I was about two years away from becoming the perfect teacher. Lunnie looked at me as if that statement were ridiculous. He did not believe it because I am a dandy, and he thinks nothing good could come from a dandy. He was wrong.

Mall, the owner of a bar that I occasionally stopped by, said to me after my illness, "Well, we lost a good one." He seemed to be saying that we lost a good teacher. In reality, he meant that the devil missed a good sacrifice.

When talking about Silly in prison, the son of Lunnie said, "I'll guarantee he will never get out alive." A "friend" of mine talking about Silly in prison also said, "I'll guarantee you that he'll never get out alive." Of course both men were speaking about me not getting out alive. Must I be drawn a picture?

I am gaining the power to discern truth from lies. Understanding motives helps very much in understanding behavior. I am also receiving the power to control others by my thoughts. I will not go into specifics because I am only now realizing this gift.

When I was in tribulation I brought a Bible to school, and this upset the Satanists very much. Also, about this time I went to hear Bill Glass preach. He said, "Give the devil your best shot first." I went up to Glass, who was a professional football player, and said, "You are a very good football player. I have seen you on TV." He did not recognize my comment in any way; he turned his back to me. In this way he robbed me of any pleasure I might have had in pleasing him.

The Civil War has always been of interest to me. Here is a quotation by Gibbons (1810-1892)–"We are coming Father Abraham, three hundred thousand more." Are the 300,000 Rights? Which Abraham is Gibbons talking about? Abraham the patriarch? Abraham the president? Both?

I highly suspect that the Civil War took place, at least partly, to do away with dandies. At Gettysburg there were 25,000 Confederate and 8,000 Union troops killed. It has been said that the Civil War was fought over slavery. It was: chattel slavery.

I might add that the Japanese, being a spiritual people, are obsessed with the American Civil War.

This brings up a question: since I am a dandy, why was I not sent to Vietnam? Another question: if the Rights consider themselves righteous, would they not be self-righteous?

MILTON–"The mind is a place of its own. It can make a hell of heaven and a heaven of hell."

Where is heaven? Is it here today? What about the many mansions? Are they here also? What about the streets of gold? Are they here also? Liquid gold—oil, asphalt?

Taking a test in college is a farce. The professor can make the dandy score whatever he wants him to score. He can lock his mind or unlock his mind at will. The professor would make a good Gypsy.

This next concept is very controversial: should the ends, if noble enough, justify the means? This concept is termed Machiavellian. Many people believe in this concept, but invariably it leads to a police state.

The following happened to me between tribulations. Silly, my tormentor, was very much on my mind. It was only a few weeks after I escaped from the Satanists. I decided to go to a U.N.C. football game. I called my "friend" Karol and invited him to go to the game, saying I would buy the tickets. He said that he would go. I very much needed someone to lean on at the time.

When I arrived at his house he had changed his mind and was not going with me. I could not change his mind. When I entered the stadium, I went to a place I always go. The first people that I saw were Silly and Sobby, two serial killers. This made me very nervous. I left.

A few days later Karol asked me if I had seen Silly lately. Then several times in the following weeks he asked me the same question. I realized that something very strange was happening here. There seemed to be some sort of connection between Karol and Silly.

Many years earlier, Karol would say to me, "Ain't nothing going to happen to you and the little orphan Annie." There was a character in this comic strip called "thing." "Thing" looked very much like me. Many times I have been referred to as "that thing."

When I was in tribulation and talking on the phone, people would end their sentences with a hiss (air between the teeth). This unnerved me at the time, but I have since understood completely.

I do not for an instant underestimate the power of Satan. I have come to realize that Satan controls many Christians.

Many Rights have contempt for their own bodies. For instance, when they use the phrase "whip my ass." Here they are degrading their own bodies. Here are a few more such terms:

"Hello." This is an expression used when a Right greets a dandy. *Hell* means exactly that, and *O* means eternity.

"Hey!" Here is another greeting that Rights use on dandies. This really means *hay*, food for the jackasses.

"Hi." Here is yet another one used by the Rights on dandies. Hi could mean up. (The sun?)

DAVIS–"I climbed and, step by step, O Lord ascended into hell."

The Rights, from the word go, know that dandies are headed for hell. Something is a little different about this unit, however. I might mention that I have seen the devil at the mental health center on two occasions. Of course, the devil is a spirit, and it doesn't say much to talk about bodies.

The spiritual bank of people's thoughts and actions (life histories of dandies) is available for Christians and Satanists alike.

Many times the Rights have pumped me full of bullshit. I understand the motive behind it. Can what happened to me happen to you? No. You must be a dandy for it to happen to you.

During induced tribulation I wanted to sound the alarm to everyone. It didn't work. The Rights were laughing up their sleeves.

Creationism has always been of interest to me. Most Christians believe strongly in creationism. I believe in creationism also. The critical aspect of creationism is time. If God created this world, does it matter how long he took? As long as we are here, does it matter how we got here? Organic evolution may be God's method of justifying present day life.

I had an uncle whom I loved very much. I'll call him Uncle Fice. He was a contractor and gave me much work when I was a teenager. He was my godfather. He always treated me very well. Sometimes he would get drunk, and on those occasions he would tease me. He would sometimes say, "I have discovered what you are good for. Changing light bulbs." Also he would say: "Why can't you be like Jay?" Jay was my age and the son of Fice's best friend. Jay won the Amateur Golf Championship in North Carolina. Uncle Fice thought that he must take me under his wing; it was his duty. I was an albatross around his neck.

Once at my father's house I was in great tribulation. It was dark and I was getting into my car and my father got into my car also. Was it my father? I felt my father's forearm, and it was very hairy, extremely hairy. The arm was much too hairy to be my father's. I began to drive very fast, with no lights. At a stoplight, whoever was in the car with me jumped out.

Also, on a trip to my father's house, my father put fear into my heart many times. I headed home in my Mustang. I was on an unfamiliar road and I opened up the Mustang. The devil was in the back seat. I ran out of road. I crashed in a grove of small trees. I did not get a scratch on me. If I had crashed a couple of feet to the right, my bumper would have caught the bank and I would have died instantly.

The god of most Rights persecutes the dandies. This is one reason why I must not recognize the god of the Rights as the one true god. Their god is not my god.

There is also the strategy of lulling the dandy to sleep. Give him enough rope and he will hang himself.

Who is more valuable to society? Silly or Tim? Silly fits very well into society. He executes people who are, by and large, non-spiritual and non-productive. This is the creed of the Satanists. Society does a little executing also.

The finer points of organic evolution are apparent to me, but what about spiritual evolution? What about survival of the fittest in the spiritual world? Is one spirit crowding out the other spirits? How do spirits multiply?

The Rights control me most of the time. I am very much aware of this fact. I am not strong enough yet to rid myself of subliminal influences. I am beginning to make a little headway in this area.

Was Mark Twain the devil? Mark Twain means 12 feet. (Under?) Mark simply means a sucker. Much of his works tell how to destroy a dandy. It is very hard to accept the extent of Satanism.

Confessions of a Dandy

When in the U.S. Army I fired "expert" with the M-14 rifle. Only 9 of us out of 250 troops fired at this level. Through the years I have had the occasion numerous times to tell people that I fired "expert" in the army. No one ever acknowledges that fact; there is no credit for the dandies.

Sentimentality is an emotion. It can also be described as feelings or as romantic or nostalgic emotion. The Rights control sentimentality in the dandies by words, body posture (including facial expressions), and simple projection.

My mother, as I was growing up, would tell me not to play with certain people because they were bad. She tried to make me believe that I was a superior person, and she succeeded, to some extent. It took me forty-five years to recognize this as hokum. The people that she projected as bad were, in fact, very good people.

I know that my life's history is with me. Is it in my mind, or is it in my brain, the physical part of my mind? This bank of knowledge must have a location, but where? Above the head? Or is it that awful unseen power?

The Rights make up the rules of life as they go along. I am learning to trust my heart rather than my senses. The Rights try to keep me in the physical world, but their methods are losing power.

Most people have a hierarchy of the importance of the different kinds of life. They even have a hierarchy within species, man in particular. People who breed animals for certain traits have a hierarchy of desirability of these traits. This process is called artificial selection when man does the selecting instead of nature.

Some people believe that all life is sacred. Mahatma Gandhi would not step on an ant.

Sitting in a chair in a beauty shop recently, I looked in the mirror and noticed my front teeth missing. There were three women in the shop. Everything was quiet. All of a sudden, I thought, *God knocked my teeth out.* At that instant the beauty shop became alive with laughter and rejoicing.

Psalms 3:7

"Arise, O Lord; save me O my God: For thou hast smitten all mine enemies upon the cheekbone; thou hast broken the teeth of the ungodly."

I was drunk when I fell and broke my teeth. I was smitten on the cheekbone by both of my wives. Now, if God were in these wives, it could be said that God smote me on the cheekbone. I am not at all sure about this.

Some people have very strong spirits, for example, Rev. Moon, the Pope, and many others who are toward the top of different religions, creeds, and cults. How these people attain this spiritual power I do not understand.

There is a line of thought that states that everything in the universe is somehow connected to everything else in the universe.

When I was in tribulation, my mother and I went to Chapel Hill. We saw in the window of a men's shop an unbelievable looking pair of pants. They were very loud, with clashing colors on a patchwork quilt. Mom wanted to buy them for me, but the old dandy had become too old for that.

I believe that spirits control animals, dogs in particular. I did at one time believe that it was a smart dog that obeyed his master. Now I realize that it is the master's spiritual power that causes the dog to be smart.

Do spirits have mass and take up space? I do not know the answer to this, but I do know that somehow they control people. I also believe that they can pass through at least some physical barriers. Whether they can materialize or become visible I do not know, but I suspect that they can; spectres.

Whether spectres are where they appear to be (life size, about ten or fifteen feet away), I do not know. What is more rational is that the spectres are somehow formed in the optic centers of the cerebrum.

A "friend" once told me, "If you are ever charged with drunk driving or an offense where drinking is involved, do not ever put a drunk on the jury. He will convict you every time." This happened to me; I was the drunk on the jury. I was the first juror to vote guilty in a drunk driving case. The state had a weak case, and in the end we found him not guilty. I remembered what my friend said. The moral of this is not to be quick to judge.

Can art be pornographic? This is a tough one, but I believe true art cannot be pornographic. The criterion is whether it induces lust in the beholder.

What about the term "German"? *Germ* means the physical spark of life (physical). *Man* means the spiritual spark of life.

Almost everything in the English language can be taken more than one way.

I am well aware that my problems are not all external. I have much evidence that some of my problem is internal. I will not expound on this because I am just now coming to grips with it. There are some truths about myself that I do not know, and the Rights are sure as hell not going to tell me. They would have me believe anything but the truth.

While in the army, I had a supplement sent to my mother. For two years I thought my mother was receiving it, but she was not. Twenty-five years later I discovered that my mother had not received one cent. Someone in payroll got it. How was I prevented from checking with my mother about the money?

I have desperately struggled for my sanity. No one can ever imagine what I have been through. The Rights were—and are—working against me. People are beginning to pay some attention to me, however. I am becoming like the elephant in the living room, hard to ignore. If I could change anything in my life, I would not change one whit. If my life history were changed even minutely, I would be dead and in hell. Now I am going in the other direction.

PART 5

Notes on Revelation

I can relate to the Book of Revelation. Doubtless much which is, by design, obscure to us in this book will be clear to those for whom it was written as the time approaches. It is, therefore, a prophecy.

2 Peter 1:20

"Knowing this first, that no prophecy of the scripture is of any private interpretation."

Revelation 1:16

"And he had in his right hand seven stars: and out of his mouth went a sharp two edged sword."

Revelation 1:20

"The seven stars are the angels of the seven churches: and the seven candlesticks which thou sawest are the seven churches."

It can be no doubt that the sword that came out of his mouth is words. Christ?

Revelation 1:18

"Behold, I am alive for evermore, Amen; and have the keys of hell and of death."

This verse seems to imply that only God can cast people into hell. This also implies that he has the keys of death.

There follows a discussion of the messages to the seven churches, in terms of the way the messages to the seven churches apply to my personal experiences.

THE MESSAGE TO EPHESUS

Revelation 2:2

"I know thy works, and thy labor, and thy patience, and how thou canst not bear them which are evil: And thou hast tried them which say they are apostles and are not, and hast found them liars."

I cannot bear "them which are evil." I have discovered that almost all of the so-called born again Christians are liars.

BLAKE—"The truth told with ill intent beats all the lies you can invent."

Revelation 2:4

"Nevertheless I have somewhat against thee, because thou hast left thy first love."

The first love is the pursuit of truth. I will never leave it again.

Revelation 2:6

"But this thou hast, that thou hatest the deeds of the Nicolaitanes, which I also hate."

This is a very interesting verse. I believe that the fact that my state psychiatrist is a Dr. Nicola is more than coincidence. The word "Nicolaitanes" is derived from the Greek *nikao*, meaning to conquer, and *loas*, meaning the people or laity. There is no ancient authority for a sect of the Nicolaitanes. If the word is symbolic, it refers to the earliest form of the notion of a priestly order, or clergy, which later divided an equal brotherhood into priests and laity.

Again, I must point out that this could be an ancient reference to the difference between Rights and Lefts. I also believe that the deeds of the Nicolaitanes are the methods used today in psychology, political science and sociology. People who have mental illness have, in reality, spiritual illness. The Rights carefully conceal this from the Lefts, although not all patients are Lefts. Nevertheless I cannot understand the connection between the brain (physical) and the mind (spiritual).

Revelation 2:7

"He that hath an ear, let him hear what the spirit saith unto the churches; to him that overcometh will I give to eat of the tree of life, which is in the midst of the paradise of God."

THE MESSAGE TO SMYRNA

Revelation 2:9-10

"I know thy works, and tribulation, and poverty (but thou art rich) and I know the blasphemy of them which say they are Jews, and are not, but are the synagogue of Satan.

"Fear none of those things which thou shalt suffer: Behold the devil shall cast some of you in prison, that ye may be tried; and ye shall have tribulation ten days: be thou faithful unto death, and I will give thee a crown of life."

"But thou art rich" could mean spiritually rich. It could mean physically rich. I am an only child and my mother is fairly wealthy. I am poor.

The synagogue of Satan stands for most born again Christians in general and the Gideons and such in particular. The devil cast me into prison for ten days and I had great tribulation. I prayed to God continually and he saved me. God has given me great courage; I fear nothing.

Revelation 2:11

"He that hath an ear, let him hear what the spirit saith unto the churches; he that overcometh shall not be hurt of the second death."

THE MESSAGE TO PERGAMOS

Revelation 2:12-15

"And to the angel of the church in Pergamos write: These things saith he which hath the sharp sword with two edges; I know thy works. And where thou dwellest, even where Satan's seat is: and thou holdest fast my name, and hast not denied my faith, even in those days wherein Antipas was my faithful martyr, who was slain among you, where Satan dwelleth.

"But I have a few things against thee, because thou hast there them that hold the doctrine of Balaam, who taught Balac to cast a stumbling block before the children of Israel, to eat things sacrificed unto idols, and to commit fornication.

"So hast thou also them that hold the doctrine of the Nicolaitanes, which thing I hate."

Balaamism is nothing more than worldliness. Satan's seat is the world. Here again we have the Nicolaitanes, whose doctrine God hates—treating spiritual problems as mental problems.

"He that hath an ear, let him hear what the spirit saith unto the churches; to him that overcometh will I give to eat of the hidden manna and will give him a white stone, and in the stone a new name written, which no man knoweth saving he that receiveth it."

The Message to Thyatira

Revelation 2:18-25

"And unto the angel of the church in Thyatira write: These things saith the son of God, who has his eyes like unto a flame of fire, and his feet are like fine brass; I know thy works, and charity, and service, and faith, and thy patience, and thy works; and the last to be more than the first.

"Not withstanding I have a few things against thee, because thou sufferest that woman Jezebel, which calleth herself a prophetess, to teach and to seduce my servants to commit fornication, and to eat things sacrificed unto idols. And I gave her space to repent of her fornication; and she repented not. Behold, I will cast her into a bed, and them that commit adultery with her into great tribulation, except they repent of their deeds. And I will kill her children with death; and all the churches shall know that I am he which searcheth the reins and hearts; and I will give unto everyone of you according to your works.

"But unto you I say, and unto the rest in Thyatira, as many as have not this doctrine, and which have not known the depths of Satan, as they speak; I will put upon you none other burden. But that which ye have already, hold fast till I come."

I began this book with "What is Truth?" and draw nigh to the end with "Notes on Revelation." The last is more than the first. Jezebel is mentioned here because in the Old Testament Jezebel attempted to mix the Jewish religion with the religion of the Phoenicians—heathenism.

The fornication mentioned is spiritual fornication. Some scholars believe that Jezebel is symbolic of the Catholic Church, where most any sin can be routinely forgiven. There is a possibility, also, that this refers to the physical act.

Revelation 2:17

"And he that overcometh and keepeth my works unto the end, to him will I give power over the nations: And he shall rule them with a rod of iron; as the vessels of a potter shall they be broken to shivers; even as I received of my father. And I will give him the morning star. He that hath an ear, let him hear what the spirit saith unto the churches."

The morning star is Venus, goddess of beauty.

MESSAGE TO SARDIS

Revelation 3:1-5

"And unto the angel of the church in Sardis write: These things saith he that hath the seven spirits of God, and the seven stars; I know thy works, that thou hast a name that thou livest and art dead.

"Be watchful and strengthen the things which remain, that are ready to die: For I have not found thy works perfect before God. Remember therefore how thou hast received and heard, and hold fast and repent. If therefore thou shalt not watch, I will come on thee as a thief, and thou shalt not know what hour I will come upon thee.

"Thou hast a few names even in Sardis which have not defiled their garments; and they shall walk with me in white: For they are worthy."

Sardis means "those who have escaped."

Here is the second time that the Lord speaks of his approaching advent: "I will come on thee as a thief."

Revelation 3:5-6

"He that overcometh, the same shall be clothed in white raiment; and I will not blot out his name out of the book of life, but I will confess his name before my father, and before his angels.

"He that hath an ear, let him hear what the spirit saith unto the churches."

MESSAGE TO PHILADELPHIA

Revelation 3:7-11

"And to the angel of the Church in Philadelphia write: These things saith he that is holy, he that is true, he that hath the key of David, he that openeth, and no man shutteth; and shutteth, and no man openeth; I know thy works: behold, I have set before thee an open door, and no man can shut it; for thou hast a little strength, and hast kept my word, and hast not denied my name.

"Behold, I will make them of the synagogue of Satan, which say they are Jews, and are not, but do lie; behold I will make them to come

and worship before thy feet, and to know that I have loved thee. Because thou has kept the word of my patience, I also will keep thee from the hour of temptation, which shall come upon all the world, to try them that dwell upon the earth.

"Behold I come quickly: hold that fast which thou hast that no man take thy crown."

The word Philadelphia means "brotherly love." The key of David could be Christ himself. Who are these people in the synagogue of Satan who say they are Jews but do lie? Who will worship before whose feet?

Case scenario: I was a Left, a non-spiritual person, and I joined a church. I thought that I was a Christian (Jew, in this case); I would sometimes answer an altar call. I would kneel at the feet of the preacher. Now the preacher knew that I was not a Christian (Jew), but I did not know it; I considered myself a Christian. So the preacher thinks that I am the synagogue of Satan because I said that I was a Jew and was not. What kind of hokum is this? He and his Christian friends are actually the synagogue of Satan.

Revelation 3:12-13

"Him that overcometh will I make a pillar in the temple of my God, and he shall go no more out: And I will write upon him the name of my God and the name of the city of my God, which is new Jerusalem which cometh down out of heaven from my God: And I will write upon him my new name.

"He that hath an ear, let him hear what the spirit saith unto the churches."

THE MESSAGE TO LAODICEA

Revelation 3:14-19

"And unto the angel of the church of the Laodiceans write: these things saith the amen, the faithful and true witness, the beginning of the creation of God: I know thy works, that thou art neither cold nor hot: I would thou wert cold or hot. So then because thou art lukewarm, and neither cold or hot, I will spew thee out of my mouth.

"Because thou sayest, I am rich, and increased with goods, and have need of nothing: and knowest not that thou art wretched, and miserable, and poor, and blind, and naked: I counsel thee to buy of me gold tried in fire, that thou mayest be rich; and white raiment, that thou mayest be clothed, and that the shame of thy nakedness do not appear; and anoint thine eyes with eye salve, that thou mayest see.

"As many as I love, I rebuke and chasten: be zealous therefore, and repent."

In this case "amen" means so be it. I contend that it is Satan who uses the term *amen* to mean without men. "I know thy works that thou are neither cold nor hot . . . thou art lukewarm." This could refer to my work because my work is lukewarm.

"*And knowest not that thou art wretched, and miserable, and poor, and blind, and naked.*" This is the condition of most Christians' souls.

"*I counsel thee to buy of me gold tried in fire [that is, divine righteousness], that thou mayest be rich; and white raiment [that is, practical righteousness] that thou mayest be clothed; and anoint thine eyes with eye salve [that is, the anointing of the Holy Spirit], that thou mayest see.*

"*As many as I love, I rebuke and chasten.*" God has rebuked and chastened me to the limit.

Revelation 3:20-22

"*Behold I stand at the door, and knock: if any man hear my voice, and open the door, I will come in to him, and will sup with him, and he with me. To him that overcometh will I grant to sit with me in my throne, even as I also overcame, and am set down with my father in his throne. He that hath an ear, let him hear what the spirit saith unto the churches.*"

FAMILY TIES

As I mentioned earlier, we called my grandfather Uncle Pill. When I was growing up, he was my security—mentally, spiritually, and physically. He allowed me to lean on him to the fullest. He never wavered. I now realize that he had some dealings with the devil. He referred to me as a dandy. When he died it upset me very much.

DONNE–"Dull sublunary lover's love (whose soul is sense) cannot admit absence, because it doth remove those things which elemented it."

Uncle Pill was a member of the Ku Klux Klan. A relative told me this. I know it is true, for I found Ku Klux paraphernalia in his closet when I was young. Skin color has little to do with the activities of the Klan. It is open season on all Lefts.

When my first wife left me I was very depressed. I moved into Uncle Pill's big brick house and got on a drunk. Uncle Mule, who was in charge of things, moved his son out and let me move in. I wondered why he did this, but I now know that Uncle Mule thought there was a good chance of my being killed in the house.

He was right. On several occasions I was almost killed. I was the only person between the rest of the family and my mother's very modest fortune.

My old "friend" Silly actually saved my life when he tried to take it. If he had not tried to take my life and wake me up to the spiritual world, I would no doubt be dead.

BLAKE–"When the senses are shaken and the soul is driven to madness, who can stand?"

My father, who is a devout Christian, told me that Jesus could read people's minds. The case in point is "the woman taken in adultery." The Pharisees brought the woman to Jesus. They tried to trap him, but they couldn't. My father said that Jesus could read their minds.

The Christians of today can not only read the minds of Lefts— and probably each other's—but they can also put thoughts in the minds of Lefts. These thoughts are sometimes very evil. Now, if true born again Christians put evil thoughts in the minds of men, I want none of it.

The Christians look down on people who drink or smoke, considering them sinful. But they do things far worse, and somehow they are forgiven. Playing with somebody's mind is a greater sin than killing him.

The trials that Jesus and other Biblical Christians went through were not experienced by modern Christians, with good reason. How do Rights possess so much knowledge? They are in tune with the spiritual. They can draw from a multitude of souls.

The Gettysburg Undress

THE GETTYSBURG UNDRESS

"Fourscore and seven years ago our fathers [spiritual fathers] brought fourth on this continent a new nation ["Rights"] conceived in Liberty, and dedicated to the proposition that all men [mankind] are created equal.

Now we are engaged in a great Civil War, testing whether that nation ["Rights"], or any nation so conceived and so dedicated, can long endure.

We are met on a great battlefield of that war. We have come to dedicate a portion of that field, as a final resting place for those who here gave their lives [physical] that the nation ["Rights"] might live.

It is altogether fitting and proper that we should do this. But in a larger sense [spiritual], we cannot dedicate—we cannot consecrate—we cannot hallow—this ground.

The brave men [man], living and dead who struggled, have consecrated it, far above our poor power to add or detract. The world [spiritual] will little note nor long remember what we say here, but it can never forget what they did here [mainly extinguish chattel slavery: kill all of the dandies possible]. It is for us the living, rather, to be dedicated here to the unfinished work which they who fought here have thus far so nobly advanced. [The unfinished work is killing the remaining dandies.] It is rather for us to be here dedicated to the great task remaining before us. [The great task is exterminating the dandies.] That from these honored dead we take increased devotion to that cause [killing the dandies] for which they gave the last full measure of devotion. That we here highly resolve that these dead shall not have died in vain. [They only died physically, not spiritually.]

That this nation [mankind], under God [?], shall have a new birth of freedom and that government of the people ["Rights"], by the people ["Rights"], for the people ["Rights"], shall not perish from the earth.

Watts ───────► "HOPE"

Confessions of a Dandy

The Spiritual Dandy

If these papers are untrue, disregard them. If they are true, heed them. These papers cannot be for my fame and fortune. People desire that I stop writing these papers. Who gets credit for these papers?

I do not have a deadline for finishing a paper. If I did, it would put pressure on me. I may paint myself into a corner. I have discovered that time can work for or against a person. I sometimes think I am mentally ill, and sometimes I think I am sane. (No one is completely sane.)

The thoughts in my papers cannot always be put into good syntax, but each paper has a kind of closure. I feel that I represent all men (not mankind).

An old professor told me that every thought that men could think has already been thought. If this is true, the human mind is finite. It is true that all of the combinations of positions on a chess board approach infinity, but in fact they are finite. I cannot accept a finite human mind, but I can accept my psyche being placed in a computer. Beware computer, this dandy is a very good chess player.

Are Rights influencing these papers? I think that they have tried, with very little success.

Here is something that applies to everyone: intelligence intimidates.

Throughout my life I had too much faith in the human mind and not enough faith in God. I know that I must be brave, because I know that I am taking on the devil. I feel melancholy about Rights. I know that there is a chink in their armor, much like a crack in the Liberty Bell. God has not been with me through all of my experiences for nothing. One work that he desires me to do is expose the hypocrites.

Everybody has at least a small death wish. It is usually in the unconscious part of the psyche. People who smoke and drink have a much stronger death wish than those who do not smoke and drink. When the Satanists attempted to sacrifice me, they knew what they were doing. I had a very strong, sublimated death wish. Even after I escaped from them I kept my death wish. I would get drunk and go to bars late at night, just begging to be killed. The Satanists knew this, and on several occasions they tried to oblige me. I do not know as fact, but I believe, that the Satanists cannot kill unless they can induce fear.

My life has undergone a type of metamorphosis. The albatross is becoming a phoenix. I have, quite literally, come back from the dead. There are several men whom I would have trusted with my life, who have attempted to kill me.

The Satanists that are open, such as the K.K.K., Skinheads, and Nazis, are not to be feared. The ones to be watched are certain covert Satanists who pass themselves off as Christians. The God of this earth is not the real thing.

The Civil War worked to eliminate slavery in two ways: it freed the physical slaves and killed the chattel slaves. This country was built on the backs of both of these types of slaves.

Attempts to drive me insane worked for years, but God stepped in and put a stop to it. God does not let me know what I want to know, but what I need to know. Some things that are apparent to me are unknown to other people. There are subliminal messages that turn my conscious mind on and off. I am working very hard to decipher these stimuli.

Dandies are immediately recognized by Rights. How does this happen? I suspect that the identities of Rights are, at least partially, visible in the area above their heads. Dandies lack this spirit above the head. When Rights are together they engage in all sorts of spiritual communications. The bodies of Rights are little more than vehicles through time.

Milton's *understood war* is a spiritual war; a sublimated war between Rights and Lefts—see Ephesians, 6:12. God will let me know when and if I am to take the initiative. He is giving me tremendous power. My faith in my god is stronger than the Rights' faith in their god. How did I arrive at this statement? When the rights pray to their god, they expect their god to answer their prayers overtly and soon. They must have constant reinforcement from their god or they will lose faith.

My god answers my prayers in a very subtle manner. I would not dare ask him for anything physical. He gives me what I need. He has revealed to me that he will destroy anything that would harm me. No one is quite sure how to handle me. God will not let me surrender. There will be no resting on laurels or illusions or grandeur. He takes care of me better than I know. The Rights are hurt by their own poison. When they put pressure on me, I know that I am getting to them. The pressure takes something out of them, also. Satan has used about all of his tricks on me. People are tired of praying for my demise. Their god versus my god.

In the eighteenth century there was an engraver in England named William Hogarth. He engraved a series of prints which could best be described as social satires. One of his most popular engravings is "The Shrimp Girl." Hogarth despised what man has done to man (or more correctly, what man has done to men). And his engravings show the human animal as no other artist has since his time.

The thing that man has done to men is this: make dandies. The Rights hate the dandies for being what they made them. The sad thing about the dandies is that they are chattel slaves and do not know it.

I am a spiritual dandy, which is very, very unusual—maybe unique. The term "dandy" is seldom used in speech or in writings, but the dandy himself is recognized . . . by Rights. The Rights don't understand me. They try to exploit my weaknesses. They are having trouble finding them. I have no fear, anger, envy, jealousy, or the nature of the spendthrift or hoarder. I do have compassion and the most powerful trait of all, love.

You may think that the normal thing to do is to hate back when you are hated. If I only prayed for those who love me I would pray for no one.

Here is hucksterism with another twist. A man about my age ran a store that I frequented. I would be the only person in the store besides him. When he would go outside to pump some gas and return, he would count his money. This happened many times. The motive for this behavior is not that he thought I would steal the money, but to make me think that he thought that I would steal the money. The same behavior can occur at work and nearly any other endeavor.

The secrets (ways and means) are carefully kept from the dandies. I truly believe that I am on the verge of elucidating these secrets, with power from God.

The only way someone gives me something is if they expect more from me in return. I think that the Rights are fiddling while Rome burns, or at the least they are whistling in the graveyard. The constant series of traps that the Rights set for me are mostly ineffective. The reason for this is that I know what they think I don't know, and I don't know what they think I know.

I can't imagine anyone giving me anything that would help me spiritually. However, the Rights underestimate my source of knowledge. A person must distinguish between thoughts from God and thoughts from Satan, good thoughts and evil thoughts, if you please. If your thoughts are mostly evil, you have some work to do. If your thoughts are mostly good, you also have some work to do.

An old man once told me, "Expect nothing and you will not be disappointed." However, we must expect some things. These things are called hope. I have been disappointed many times.

I have very little social life. I like it like that. At one time I craved being around people. Now I am quite content being alone. I remember Robert Burns' definition of society, "Studied in the arts of hell in wickedness refined."

What about aliens here in the United States? I believe that the aliens in this country are in the majority. I call them Rights. It is much like you can't see the trees for the forest. Who is fooling whom? The poor dandies see nothing. The spiritual power of the Rights can cause the dandies to believe anything.

It helps to know your enemies, it also helps to know your friends—if, indeed, you have any. As I become more and more aware of spiritual laws, I do not like what I see. In all sorts of speech I can immediately determine the motive behind a statement.

There are several people whom I love dearly. They are Rights. I am not fooled, although in a way I want to be fooled.

The dandies: where are they? I believe the Rights are keeping the dandies away from me. This is only a guess, however. I am aware that Rights, for the most part, must obey certain spiritual laws. I am ignorant of these laws for the most part, but I know more now than I did in the past. I inadvertently give away much information, but the Rights also reveal much information inadvertently. This is about the only way I can receive truth from Rights.

One weakness on my part is to quickly answer questions that are posed to me, almost like a reflex. I have tried to change myself in this regard. Now I ponder questions that are asked of me and try to decipher the motive. Sometimes when I am in a conversation, I am not in control of my speech. Sometimes the spirit controls my speech, and it upsets people. When this takes place I am barely conscious of what I have said. It is true that I must not in the least be vindictive.

Reincarnation. I will not discuss this word but simply ask why it is seldom used. Most of the Bible is based on the term. Much of English literature is based on this term. What is the secret? Is there something to fear? If reincarnation is indeed true, human bodies are no more than vehicles through time. There is a theory called "continuity of germ plasm" that is the physical equivalent of reincarnation.

I have an old dog. I love this dog more than almost anything. For a brief period of time I thought that a certain person had deliberately run over my dog. I literally had murder in my heart. I prayed for God to remove it from my heart, and he did. Then he revealed to me that it was not at all as I had imagined. I even had the wrong man. Also it is easier, much, much easier, to forgive than to hold a grudge.

Being a dandy, and somewhat understanding the spiritual aspects of things, where do I fit in? Where does a dandy who understands the Gettysburg Address—and much more—fit into the scheme of things? What about the American way?

The fact that I have worked hard and am fairly intelligent is the only reason I got a small piece of the pie. Now, do the Rights, who run everything, view me as a threat? I have little physical evidence to support this idea, but my heart says this is true.

Why would I desire to upset a situation that is going so well for me? I will tell you what it is. It can be summed up in the phrase, "the pursuit of truth." God will not let me rest until I obtain this truth. The Rights are afraid that they will lose their spiritual superiority, and they are right (no pun intended).

Now for a little truth in music. Each of the keys of the scale has its own characteristics. Otherwise all music would be written in one key. In modern music some peculiar things take place. First of all is backward masking. This occurs when a subliminal message is placed on a tape. There is also something strange happening sometimes when a song is sung in harmony. The same consonants in some of the words are not sung by all of the harmony. For example, one may hear "Lucy in disguise" or "Lucy in the skies."

Either can be heard.

If I work hard and master a difficult piece of music, I am tired of it by then.

I will say this, I am a slow learner, but when I learn something, I learn it better than anyone else. An old professor told me, "Experience is the best teacher, but it is the only teacher that fools understand."

I have a feeling that the Rights know more about who I am than I know myself. I remember very well what they have done to me. The term "nigger" is interchangeable with the term "dandy."

Once I attended a church with a friend of mine. I was in tribulation and very much in need of someone to lean on. This Christian church, I thought, might be the answer. I sat in the congregation and looked at the choir. A choir member had a pocket watch which he swung back and forth like a pendulum. This vexed me. Don't tell me about good Christian this and good Christian that. As far as I can tell they are all in the synagogue of Satan.

When I was young, my father would take me to tent meetings. These tent meetings were complete with a carnival atmosphere, sawdust on the floor and a calliope for music. Once the jackleg preacher told the people to spare the rod and spoil the child. My father went directly home and beat the hell out of me, for no reason whatsoever.

When I am conversing with Rights, they will not let me prove a point. They interrupt my speech, and if I do make a point they disagree vehemently, saying, "No, no! That is not right."

With some endeavors that I undertake, I am pathetic, but no more pathetic than the efforts of the Rights to influence my behavior. They truly insult my intelligence.

Many people who write poetry use the word "God" carelessly. It is a word that is very much overused. It is much as if there is a blank space in their poetry, so they just plug the word "God" into their writings. This type of writing could best be described as sophomoric.

What do Satanists look like? I will tell you that some Satanists are extremely clean people. Looks can be very deceiving. What does God look like? I have no idea, but I know that both God and Satan work through people.

What about electricity? I strongly suspect that spirits are some type of electricity. If this is true, can electricity be alive? I have seen Satan dematerialize. Where does electricity fit into this process?

Electrons can be viewed as fundamental building blocks of atoms. Under normal conditions all chemical reactions are dependent upon electrons.

Through the years I have had a difficult time being understood. Even intelligent people could not understand me. I could seldom use my intelligence because no one could understand me. Some parts of my mind could not be put into language.

Many Rights put on an air of superiority. I can see right through it. I am beginning to understand some of the parameters of the spiritual world, but the paradigm remains mostly a mystery.

Supposedly, the Christians worship the good part of the psyche of man and the Satanists worship the evil in a man's psyche. Put them together and you have closure of the human psyche.

Do Rights know the truth about human evolution? It is obvious that there are two parts to this question: the spiritual and the physical. Both of these aspects of evolution can be traced back thousands of years. One question that I ask is: Did the spirit evolve through all these years retaining its basic characteristics? Are there subtle changes occurring during the process of reincarnation? How and what are the entities added to the spirit as it passes through time?

Rights must project an air of superiority, but some Rights are as dumb as hammers. These dumb Rights still feel superior to intelligent dandies. If it were not for the spirit, they would not exist.

Every time I try to help someone, it backfires on me. Also, when I let my guard down, something happens which I later reflect on. How people know when my guard is up and when it is not up, I do not know. Can they cause my guard to drop?

All Rights are phonies. It is not words that make a liar, it is thoughts. The Rights are the ones who should feel guilt and shame. If you don't know the rules, you must go on instinct. The Rights try every way they can to undermine my security. They are having no success because I know that true security is by faith in the true God.

Finally things are beginning to work out for me.